The Velveteen Principles for Women

The Velveteen Principles for Women

Shatter the Myth of Perfection and Embrace All That You *Really* Are

Toni Raiten-D'Antonio

Health Communications, Inc.
Deerfield Beach, Florida

www.hcibooks.com

Please note—The names and identifying characteristics of therapy
clients and some others mentioned in this text have been changed
to protect their privacy.

Library of Congress Cataloging-in-Publication Data
Raiten-D'Antonio, Toni.
   The velveteen principles for women : shatter the myth
of perfection and embrace all that you really are /
Toni Raiten-D'Antonio.
     p. cm.
   ISBN-13: 978-0-7573-0561-0 (hard cover)
   ISBN-10: 0-7573-0561-X (hard cover)
    1. Women—Psychology. 2. Self-realization in women.
3. Women—Conduct of life. 4. Self-actualization (Psychology)
I. Title.
HQ1206.R35 2007
158.082—dc22

                                        2006033443

HCI, its logos and marks are trademarks of Health Communications, Inc.

Publisher: Health Communications, Inc.
            3201 S.W. 15th Street
            Deerfield Beach, FL 33442-8190

Cover and inside design by Larissa Hise Henoch
Inside book formatting by Lawna Patterson Oldfield

For Amy and Elizabeth
(and every other woman struggling to stay *Real*)

CONTENTS

Contents

ACKNOWLEDGMENTS

My debt to Margery Williams and her beautiful Velveteen Rabbit is plain to see in these pages. But I have also depended on many others for inspiration and support. I am grateful for the privilege of honoring them here.

I would never have the opportunity to share what I have learned and connect with readers were it not for a wonderful group of people at Health Communications, Inc. I am grateful that Peter Vegso and Tom Sand recognized the power of the bunny from the start, and continue to value it. They have offered me both support and a level of respect that far exceeds what one might expect in a publisher/author relationship. On a day-to-day basis, Michele Matriciani, Erin Brown, Carol Rosenberg, Larissa Hise Henoch, Paola Fernandez-Rana, Ariana Falerni, Kelly Maragni, Kim Weiss, and Pat Holdsworth have been Real collaborators.

As before, David McCormick and his colleagues at McCormick & Williams have provided me with reassurance and aid, but this time they went a step further to connect me with editor David Groff. He pushed me further than I expected to go with this book by repeatedly uttering the most terrifying words ever: "I have just a few general questions."

Others who have taught me what it means to be Real include my psychotherapy clients, students, and academic colleagues. Although some may see bits and pieces of themselves in these pages, it's important to note that to assure confidentiality, names and other elements of case studies and anecdotes in my text have been altered.

The *Venus of Willendorf* has been an inspiration in my struggles to understand a woman's essential beauty. I will always admire her unadorned honesty.

My thanks to Candace Jordan, who reminded me of mask work in Real treatment.

I am indebted to the women of the Empire State College Long Island Center, especially Dr. Yvonne Murphy, whose friendship and support are evident in many of these pages.

I especially thank my daughters, the most precious Real women in my world, and my husband, Michael, without whom there would be no Velveteen Principles books.

WOMEN, RABBITS, AND BEING REAL

'm looking at a brittle and faded black-and-white photo that is more than forty-five years old. It is a picture of me at age four. My brown hair is bobbed, and I peer through big, thick eyeglasses. I sit alone atop a boulder in a suburban yard, wearing a little summer blouse with appliquéd balloons. Around my hips I've wrapped a cream-colored, lushly fringed shawl. I strike a flirty, pinup pose: head back, chest out, one hand on my hip, the other behind my head.

Moments before the picture was taken, my parents had discovered me prancing around the house, swiveling my hips to imitate the walks of the grown women I saw on TV. (My favorites were Marilyn Monroe, Olive Oyl, and Betty Boop. Though Olive wasn't curvy, she was very appealing to Popeye and Bluto.) They had brought me outside where the neighbors and anyone passing in a car could see and posed me for posterity. I did what they asked, even though I felt humiliated by the fact that they thought I was cute and not the sexy woman I was pretending to be.

Even at that young age I was desperately confused and bewildered by the prospect of becoming the kind of woman my family and the larger society seemed to value. On the one hand, I was expected to nurture others. Indeed, according to family legend, my parents made this clear when they first brought me home from the hospital and announced to my brothers, "This is Toni. She's going to take care of us." But on the other hand, the main fantasy the culture offered to little girls promised that I could escape the caretaker role if I became beautiful and sexy so that I would attract a man who would love me and support me forever. This achievement would bring my parents' approval. It was also the one sure way for me to safely leave them for a life that would be secure, comfortable, and respectable.

In the photo, the look in my eyes reminds me that even as a child I already suspected I would fall short of the fantasy. As my father held up the camera and I posed, I understood that he and my mother were seeing not Marilyn, Olive, or Betty, but an awkward little girl. Still, where they saw play, I considered myself to be learning and practicing the secrets of happy womanhood.

The Princess Paradigm

Although I couldn't have known it at the time, I was not alone in my insecurity. If you are a woman who grew up in the 1950s, you likely have a photo, or many photos, similar to the one of me posed on the boulder. If you don't have a picture, then you surely have memories of this kind of play. It is the work of childhood to spend hours pretending to be adult. For boys in my era, this meant playing cops and robbers, army, or firemen. (Each role was action-based and allowed for pretend achievements and victories.) For girls, play involved a lot of dressing up (of themselves and Barbie dolls) and trying to look pretty in a very specific way—a princess ready to be recognized and redeemed by a prince.

The style of play that prepares children for adult roles is different for every generation. And fortunately, other than marrying well, today's girls have career opportunities; they can look to role models that didn't exist in the past, including astronauts, professional athletes, and leaders in every profession. But it pains me to report from my work as a psychotherapist that it is still very common, universal really, for girls to focus a huge amount of time and energy on learning not how to be themselves, but how to be generically beautiful and sexy.

You know this generic version of the ideal woman: She is young, tall, and thin to the point of being gaunt. She has long, straight hair, preferably blonde, and blemish-free skin. Remarkably, although she's so thin, she also has large, firm, high breasts, which she displays whenever possible. She must walk, talk, and pose in a way that suggests sexual energy. She mustn't appear overly intelligent or else she'll be intimidating, and she shouldn't show too much interest in expressing herself or developing autonomy outside the realm of sex and beauty.

In both appearance and behavior, she is a lot like the world's most popular doll, Barbie, who would measure 39–18–33 if she were human. Because material wealth is also part of the ideal package, like Barbie, the perfect woman should have fashionable clothes, a beautiful house, an expensive car, and everything else money can buy.

The standards for the ideal woman are widely held and communicated in television, movies, and magazines. They associate a very narrow definition of perfection with becoming a secure woman who will be cared for by an adoring man. All girls get the message and carry it into adult life. You are affected no matter your race, income level, sexual preference, age, region, faith, intellect, talents, or goals. Even girls who aspire to become physicians, for example, talk about the need to be "hot" like the women doctors they see on TV. They dream of becoming perfectly beautiful and thereby capturing the devotion and lifelong support of a wonderful man.

I call this fantasy the Princess Paradigm. Its power was recently impressed on me by a young mother named Anne, who sees me for counseling. Anne's preschool daughter, Lily, is obsessed with princesses. She reads and re-reads books about them, watches movies that feature them, and plays at being a princess almost every day. As Anne recalled, Lily had noticed that her mother was bothered when she returned to her car in a shopping center lot to find a flat tire. "Don't worry, Mommy. You're beautiful and you're married," she had said. "Daddy will take care of you!"

As suggested by Lily's words of comfort, our culture still promises happiness and security to the woman who meets certain standards for beauty and behavior. These attributes will allow her to attract a mate and then be supported by him, just like a princess. Although expressed in different ways in modern stories, the message is basically the same one presented in classic tales such as *Cinderella, Sleeping Beauty,* and *Snow White.* Life can be a challenge, but if you are pretty enough, you will be saved. (The story that most closely fit my personal Princess Paradigm was *Cinderella* because her beauty saved her from caretaker drudgery.)

The trouble with this Princess Paradigm, beyond the fact that it insists women must be alluring and then dependent, is that very few of us can ever be sure we are pretty enough to become and remain forever a cherished princess. Therefore, we find ourselves drawn into a lifelong process of anxious mirror gazing. We struggle over the condition of our outsides—skin, hair, body—at the expense of our insides—heart, mind, soul. Worst of all, we never get the promised reward of ease, pampering, and endless admiration. Instead, as many women struggle to seem worthy, they become so committed to serving others—as mothers, partners, wives, daughters, and even as employees—that they lose themselves in the process. In the kitchen, in the bedroom, on the job, they make other people the main subject of their own lives and turn themselves into objects that exist to serve others. So many of us have this problem that one of the staples of my therapy practice involves having women clients ask the simple question: What about me? These three words instantly lead women to recognize how much they have neglected their own development and lost themselves in service to others.

I suppose the Princess Paradigm could work for a woman with movie-star looks and the time and money for the clothes, exercise, makeup, and, ultimately, frequent plastic surgery to maintain it all from adolescence to the grave. But how many of these princesses actually roam the Earth? Very few. So few, in fact, that every woman I have ever known in my roles as therapist, teacher, friend, or acquaintance has lived with the nagging sense that she is inadequate in her natural state.

By the time I was seven or eight, I suspected that I wasn't ever going to measure up to princesshood. I had bad eyesight—men don't make passes at girls who wear glasses—and I was overweight. I already felt insecure about my looks and, consequently, worried about whether I had any real worth as a person. By my teen years, I felt even worse about my appearance. High grades at school and obedience at home brought me some relief. But these rewards were small compared with my dread that I was going to be a failure in the looks department.

To fight off the self-loathing that came with feeling like I was never pretty enough, I began to study the Princess Paradigm, hoping I might discover its short-comings and feel better about failing to achieve it. I had to admit that besides beauty, the paradigm upheld values such as kindness, consideration for others, and loyalty, which are quite positive attributes. But other elements of this ideal—extreme conformity, self-censorship, and emotional/creative repression—robbed girls of life's greatest rewards. This was the price the princess had to pay. She had to abandon much of her individuality. Moreover, all that time spent on primping limited her development as a person. In the end, even the most successful princess was dependent on others for survival. The princess's life, it seemed, was a very limited kind of fantasy.

Realizing that I would never become a princess, and discovering that I didn't really want to be one after all, saved my sanity. As a child, my growing recognition helped me endure a home life that was filled with neglect and marred by occasional abuse. As an adult, this knowledge led me out of a career as a stage and TV performer (the perfect princess occupation) and into my life's work as a psychotherapist and professor. In my work, I have seen how the Princess Paradigm and other forms of social pressure limit women's lives and erode their mental health. I have also discovered positive alternatives supported by all the great theorists of human development—from Adler, Erikson, and Piaget to Kohlberg, Jung, and Maslow—who stress the value of individuality, creativity, courage, and ethical behavior. In short, they support being true to yourself. Understanding and discovery are essential for any woman who wants to pioneer her own life's course. They are also the gifts that are hidden in a children's story that presents an alternative to the Princess Paradigm. (Don't be fooled by the fact that a children's story inspired me. Life's great lessons have always been available in seemingly simple fables, myths, stories, and even songs.) That story is *The Velveteen Rabbit*.

Enter the Rabbit and the Principles

Stories, especially great children's stories, are parables that explain the adult world even as they delight us with magical characters and impossible outcomes. *The Velveteen Rabbit* by Margery Williams offers us a main character who is not a beautiful princess, but rather a raggedy stuffed bunny trapped in a world dominated by shiny mechanical toys with judgmental, conformist attitudes.

The story follows the bunny as he endures self-doubt, fear, loneliness, and sadness. Imperfect and old-fashioned–looking, the Velveteen Rabbit is nevertheless loved by a little boy who clutches him through a long and dangerous illness. And it is this love, given even though the little Rabbit is just cloth stuffed with sawdust, that gives life to the bunny. As the Rabbit's friend Skin Horse explains, "When a child loves you for a long, long time, not just to play with, but REALLY loves you, then you become Real."

In time the bunny learns to ignore the chattering criticism voiced by other toys and to appreciate himself as a flawed but beautifully unique individual who is loved.

Freed from his inhibitions and self-consciousness, and with the help of the Nursery Magic Fairy, he finally becomes Real and feels truly happy as himself.

> He gave one leap and the joy of using those hind legs was so great that he went springing about the turf on them, jumping sideways and whirling round as the others did. He was a Real Rabbit at last . . .

It's hard to overstate how much the Velveteen Rabbit longed to be Real. He recognized Realness as the main purpose of his life and a sign that he was truly loved, worthy, and special. It is also hard to overstate the value of being Real for all human beings. If we can fully accept ourselves as being valuable, worthy, and lovable, no matter how imperfect and flawed we may be, we have a chance to live as creative, empathetic, and generous people. As the Velveteen Rabbit knew, becoming Real is one of the main purposes of our lives, and it promises greater rewards than any princess can imagine.

For generations, readers have found in *The Velveteen Rabbit* a great antidote for the Princess Paradigm. The story is filled with truths that transcend age, culture, time, and place. And the more we reflect on them, the more relevant they become.

I discovered in this small story the inspiration for my first book, *The Velveteen Principles*, a guide for those who want to identify some of the sources of their unhappiness or feelings of alienation and become genuinely Real themselves. The principles include empathy, courage, honesty, generosity, gratitude, and flexibility. They remind us that it's possible for everyone to be Real, and they show us how love and ethical behavior can guide us to a life of meaning.

Of course, no book is a complete prescription for happiness, and soon after *The Velveteen Principles* was published, I began to see that it was, in a way, only the first leg of a greater journey. This was especially true for hundreds of women I met at book signings and talks. Time and again women would tell me that *The Velveteen Rabbit* was their favorite children's tale and that my book had helped them to apply the story's lessons to their own lives.

But among these women were many who said that they were having trouble becoming Real themselves, and that they were worried they would never have the kind of Real love portrayed in an anecdote I told about a loving elderly couple I saw attending to each other in my doctor's office. "I don't think I've ever loved someone like that," explained one reader tearfully, "and I sure don't think anyone loves me that way." Some readers also said that for women, the challenge of being Real was even greater than my first book acknowledged, and they wanted to continue the exploration.

With all of these comments in mind, I still wasn't fully persuaded that a special book for women was required. Then I thought about makeovers.

Makeover Mania

With so many people bringing up the same point—that women need more support for being Real—I began to think they were on to something. But it was a set of less direct comments, from women who had already read and said they shared the values expressed in *The Velveteen Principles*, that helped me to make up my mind to write this book aimed specifically at women.

Time and again, a friend, colleague, or acquaintance, hearing that I was making public appearances to discuss my book, would excitedly ask, "When are you going to get a makeover?" One magazine writer interviewing me over the phone asked, "And I suppose you've started the obligatory Botox injections for your personal appearances?"

Makeovers, now hugely popular thanks to television, plunge a woman into a sort of appearance transformation process that can include anything from a new hairstyle, clothes, and makeup to dramatic plastic surgery. Their enormous appeal confirms to me that women are subject to an ever more demanding set of standards for beauty. (If you don't think things are worse today, consider this fact: In 1985, fashion models typically weighed 8 percent less than the average woman. In 2005, they weighed 23 percent less.) It also shows how much value society places on a woman's outsides and how little we value her insides.

I was surprised that the makeover comments came from grown women who were competent, mature, and intelligent. They were successful in almost every sense of the word, and after reading my first book, they agreed that women were being limited, confined, even tyrannized by the social pressure to conform to a Generic Ideal. But as soon as they learned I might be placed in the public eye, they understood that no matter how good I felt about my book and my ideas, I would naturally feel anxious about my appearance. The implication was that I *should* get a makeover, which might allow me to look more like the cultural ideal.

Worse than my dismay about these comments was the shock I felt when I realized that part of me agreed with them. In fact, I had already wondered whether I should make a big effort to change my appearance—make myself look younger, slimmer, and more mediagenic—so that I would come closer to society's ideal. I was well aware of the social science experiments that have found pretty people are presumed to be smarter, richer, and happier than those who are not considered pretty. They are paid higher salaries and, presumably, sell more books. So, much like the little girl who had her picture taken on the boulder outside her house, I began to think that if I could make myself look a certain way, I might be rewarded.

The concern I felt about my looks, the way it made

me doubt my value and wonder whether anyone would listen to someone who looked as "average" as I do was entirely normal for a woman living in these times. The emotional and financial cost associated with today's standards for beauty are enormous; they increase every day as new styles and ideals are invented, and new products are developed to help us reach the generic goal. Today we are supposed to maintain and improve and cosmetically attend to every square inch of our bodies. Normal characteristics like cellulite are turned into shameful conditions that must be treated with a typically expensive cream or potion.

The makeover comments and my own anxiety about my appearance as I went out to discuss a book that advocates rebelling against superficiality helped me understand in a new way the power of the cultural expectations placed on all women. Think about it. The woman who has spent her life studying, analyzing, and proposing ways for people to become happy, idiosyncratic, and as Real as a well-worn Velveteen Rabbit was worried about whether she lived up to a generic, unReal ideal. And other women were worried *for* her.

I could have chosen to judge myself negatively for these feelings. But rather than criticize myself for losing sight of my own principles, I marveled at just how big an adversary we face as we try to be Real. It's quite possible we'd have a cure for cancer by now if all the hours and intelligence devoted to making women feel insecure about their looks were applied instead to medical science or other pressing social problems.

No woman I know, including myself, feels genuinely secure about her appearance and accepted by others at all times. I bet your own experience is the same. Indeed, if you listen closely to women in every realm of life, you will discover an epidemic of anxiety over issues of beauty and self-worth. Most of us are victims of this epidemic at one time or another.

We can see proof that women suffer more in the fact that depression and anxiety are twice as common among women as men. Women vastly outnumber men in my psychotherapy practice and in almost all mental health settings. Experts agree that much of the gender difference is due to the burdens placed on women around beauty, behavior, and achievement. Where do these burdens come from? The awesome and powerful combinations of social forces I call the Object Culture.

(By now you've noticed that I enjoy making up my own terms—Princess Paradigm, Object Culture—for certain concepts and ideas. These expressions help me to remember complex things and to talk about them without having to repeat complicated explanations. I also think they are helpful and fun. I hope you agree.)

The Power of the Object Culture

The organized ideas and values of a society or culture are disseminated through language, art, media, religion, commerce, and many other forms of communication. The Object Culture places high value on superficial measures of human worth—appearance, possessions, and status. Although its capital must be America, the Object Culture can be found everywhere, and as global media evolves, its reach is expanding quickly. In fact, I think it is turning the whole planet into a single cultural community—a United States of Generica, or U.S. of G. for short. In this virtual and vast dominion, happiness is defined by a one-size-fits-all lifestyle of material comfort, passivity, and a generic form of beauty that is hyper-groomed, surgically enhanced, and unblemished.

The Object Culture is so powerful and so pervasive that it is almost impossible to escape. Its messages push us to pursue perfection through whatever means necessary, but most especially by polishing our exteriors and acquiring stuff. The Object Culture even has its own harsh and superficially oriented dialect—I call it Thinglish—that is full of materialism, and reduces people to labels and stereotypes. Thinglish tells us, "You can never be too thin or too rich." Thinglish turns flesh-and-blood women into descriptors—the fat one, the widow, the sexy one. The most common and damaging way Thinglish is used to hurt women? I'd say it's referring to us as "girls" in a condescending way long after we have entered the world of adults. Who do you think gets more respect, support, and pay—the "girls" in the office or the members of the "men's club"?

According to Thinglish's definition, women are not valued unless they are both hot—meaning generically sexy—and cool. Being cool in the Object Culture means more than being up-to-date, stylish, and equipped with the most expensive clothes and electronic gadgets. In Thinglish, cool also means trying to appear aloof, indifferent, jaded, and too sophisticated to care about anything or anyone. (I recently witnessed this kind of cool in the lobby of a fancy New York hotel; no one was smiling or interacting. The people were as stiff and stuffy as the architecture. I wanted to "act out," sing a song, do a dance, even poke people to see if they were alive!)

Being cool is hugely demanding. People who are cool are always on the hunt for the newest and the latest, and they can't rest for fear of "losing" their coolness. Missing from the rhetoric of the Object Culture is the plain fact that being neither cool nor hot has a significant effect on whether we feel happy or fulfilled. The same is true of being rich or famous. After a relatively short time, lottery winners are no happier than they were before they became rich. And people who achieve fame often feel restless and let down after the attention fades. To cure this feeling, they set out to achieve more fame, with the unRealistic belief that eventually enough will be enough. It rarely is.

Because the values of the Object Culture are false, its goals can never be achieved. Just as fashions change so quickly that we can never keep up, the definition of Object Culture perfection keeps slipping farther away. Today it might be enough for you to own a big, new house and matching car. Tomorrow you'll need to add a vacation home and a boat.

The Object Culture is antithetical, corrosive, and antagonistic to mental health. It devalues emotions, individuality, and creativity. It offers one option for acceptance, shaming every person who falls outside its superficial ideal. Worst of all, it forces us to lie to the world and ourselves as we constantly act as if we are cool, hot, and in control. Indeed, many of us get so caught up in acting "as if" that we don't know what we really think and feel.

The Criticizing Voice of OPO

The values of the Object Culture are so deeply ingrained and so widely held that they shape what we think and say. This is why so many people seem to express similar judgmental statements about the people, places, and things they encounter in daily life. Object Culture values are expressed in tones of sarcasm and negativity that are familiar to us all. Women who are different and don't meet the generic ideal hear these snide and hurtful comments in the media, schools, businesses, neighborhoods, families—essentially everywhere. I call this destructive cacophony OPO for Other People's Opinions.

When I visualize OPO, who is a critical, inflexible busybody, I imagine a crazy-looking monster that sits on my shoulder shouting commands that contradict and drown out my hopes and dreams. One of my therapy clients says OPO is like a nasty neighbor. Another says OPO is a negative parent. My friend sees a marshmallow-shaped, nagging cartoon character who bounces along behind people whispering negative judgments. It's fun and useful to create an image of OPO in your mind. What does it look like to you?

Often speaking in Thinglish, OPO (pronounced oh-poh) constantly tells us what we *should* do to conform to a generic ideal, shaming us for falling short and making us feel guilty for failing. OPO judges everything about us—from our hairstyles and education levels to our creative impulses—and the "should-shame" dynamic is its favorite trick. It drives women to pursue perfection to the point of exhaustion. And it seems to be everywhere. If I stop and listen, I can hear it in my own mind:

OPO: *Why are you wasting time on this book, Toni? Your house needs cleaning, and you could do a little exercise instead of wasting your time trying to share your so-called wisdom. And* The

Velveteen Rabbit is a children's book, for Pete's sake. Grow up!

See what I mean? OPO rattles around in our heads all the time, just looking for things to criticize. But even though it's inside of us, OPO is not a natural phenomenon. Indeed, we each arrived in this world 100 percent Real, with the potential to grow into unique and happy human beings. Then OPO starts to impose on us the rules that will replace our dreams and individuality with arbitrary limits and generic roles. Most of us heard our first admonitions—"Girls don't play sports" or "Being smart will never get you a man"—from parents, grandparents, aunts and uncles, and brothers and sisters.

In my own childhood, the OPO message was clear: Girls are born to take care of other people—first a husband and children, then elderly parents. This is a script many families hand to girl children. In my case, it was amplified dramatically when my mother developed Parkinson's disease, and my father received a diagnosis of cancer. While still in elementary school, I had to take care of my parents, and my status as a "good girl" depended on how well I performed as nurse, maid, and entertainer.

Every step I took in life was supposed to be oriented

toward being a good, selfless, maintenance-free care-taker, whose main reward would be financial support first by my father, then by my husband. At school, good grades were necessary only to get me into the type of college where I might find the right kind of husband. My creative and intellectual interests were discouraged unless they could be expressed in a hobby or inconse-quential little part-time job. And every bite of food I took was monitored by my mother and father and broth-ers, all of whom feared I'd become fat and unattractive. If you are female, you likely had similar experiences with eating, so you know how they affected my self-esteem and my relationship with food. Like many of you, I have struggled with this issue my entire life.

It's no surprise that the process of becoming unReal starts with our parents and siblings. The family is where we are "socialized" to succeed, first as children and later as adults. Parents and others who train little girls to cut off parts of their personalities and channel their energies into socially acceptable interests believe they are doing the right and necessary thing. They are as much victims of OPO as the children they harm. Supposedly to "pro-tect" us, families give us a list of *shoulds* that define proper behavior so we can escape the pain of OPO. The *shoulds* include admonitions such as "Be nice or no one will like you" and "You should sacrifice yourself for others." OPO punishes us when we fail to meet its expectations. It comes in the form of shaming statements made by those we know, even love, as well as the casual comments of strangers.

"You'd be so pretty if you lost a few pounds."
"I thought for sure you'd be married by now."
"Can't you be a team player?"
"Nobody wants to hear from you right now, kid."

OPO is insidious and is often expressed in subtle and tricky ways. Take, for example, the woman who recently told me, "I'm sorry, I just lost track of what you were saying because your earrings are so distracting—there's an awful lot going on there." Her point: My earrings were ridiculous and, on behalf of OPO, she wanted to let me know, so I should feel ashamed and then guilty for distracting her. Need another example? Consider the acquaintance of mine who quipped, "Your clothes are so 'matchy-matchy' today." Here was a little more hostility in the form of OPO. Her remark forced me to go through a process of self-questioning (*Maybe I look "wrong"?*), anger (*What a bitch!*), analysis (*What's going on here?*), inhibition (*Maybe I should dress differently, so I can avoid this problem*) and then, finally, resolution (*I'm going to dress my own way and let the chips fall where they may*). What a waste of my time!

Bad as these OPO encounters may be, things get worse when we overreact and draw others into our struggle with the shaming messages. A patient of mine named Brenda reacts to her older sister's harsh and negative opinions by making a constant effort to please her. Often Brenda involves her husband and children in this dance of shame, dragging them to her sister's home for long, uncomfortable visits. They never enjoy these trips and can see that Brenda is miserable, too. But she doesn't see clearly that she is doing battle with a destructive set of messages that she would do better to ignore.

Of course, you cannot fight against OPO if you are not aware of its impact. Most of us never realize what's going on and how it affects us. Instead, we become so concerned with OPO and attuned to the content of the criticism that we know the words by heart and internalize the judging process. This usually starts as a strategy for self-protection. Frightened by OPO, we think if we judge *ourselves* harshly, maybe we can conform to social standards so perfectly that no one else will ever notice our flaws and voice a criticism.

There is a certain tragic logic to this practice. But unfortunately it almost always gets out of control. We assess and condemn ourselves countless times each day. In fact, we become so adept at self-criticism that we automatically inhibit ourselves from taking risks and expressing our individuality. At their worst, the inner judges we all carry with us can prevent us from ever being happy with our Real selves. For good measure, we then criticize ourselves for being unhappy. ("Only an idiot would be this depressed," we tell ourselves.)

Bad as these symptoms may be, the worst thing about OPO is how it can lead us to participate from both sides of the equation. We may be victims, but we are also perpetrators. Judging and criticizing are so pervasive that we begin to judge others, becoming the source of OPO for our children, friends, coworkers, and others.

OPO also has the ability to argue with us, even in our own voice. For example, I have been studying the ways that the Object Culture acts like a sexual perpetrator, manipulating us to accept more extreme definitions of acceptable behavior. I see this in the teenagers I treat who have been exposed to countless graphic sexual images. (It's a rare child who hasn't been exposed to Internet porn before he or she completes elementary school.) This imagery has an objectifying, disturbing effect. It encourages girls to be hypersexual in order to make boys like them. It trains boys to expect girls to be ever sexy, willing, and available.

OPO: *Now you're really being extreme! All of us are victims, huh? I don't buy it—we are stronger and smarter than that. We can identify the nonsense in the media and ignore it. Besides, what's wrong with being attractive? Don't you think women can be beautiful? You're being ridiculous.*

Toni: *First of all, I'm not saying we're not strong and smart. I'm saying that the Object Culture's messages are sneaky and pervasive, and we're just too busy and stressed to confront it consistently. We can be manipulated without knowing it.*

I definitely think women are beautiful, and being attractive can make us happy. But we must be free to define beauty for ourselves. The low self-esteem, self-destructiveness, chronic fear, and anxiety epidemic in today's society come from the constant bombardment of messages telling young women that unless they dress and act in a highly sexualized way, they are inadequate and ugly. OPO, you're wrong again.

Unfortunately, most of us are unaware of OPO's efforts to influence us, so we don't even argue with it. Women who unconsciously accept the rules of the Object Culture don't need to hear judgments and reminders from the outside. Instead, having internalized the culture's values they hear, and most importantly *feel*, their own hearts and minds condemn them. Judging yourself against the impossible ideal and finding yourself guilty of imperfection becomes a habit of mind. That familiar twinge of anxiety, guilt, or shame often arises without conscious thought. Women experience it as a subtle shift in mood. It happens when you step on the scale. It happens when you have a "bad hair day."

POWs

The Perfect Object Woman—or POW—has been deprived of the freedom to create her life according to her own light. She spends inordinate amounts of time and money on her appearance, but she must also be gracefully successful at everything she tries. She strives to be a glamorous, physically fit multitasker, always effectively juggling everyone else's needs. She's the soccer mom cheering on the sideline who is also a perfect housekeeper, a gourmet cook, and a tigress in the bedroom. She is so incredibly sexy that when she walks by a crowd of men, she creates a rise and fall of erections like fans doing the wave at a sporting event.

Since this is the twenty-first century, the definition of a POW often includes strict requirements for women who work. On the job, a POW is the perfect employee, June Cleaver with a clipboard, always ready to be of uncomplaining service to others—because she believes that service to others is her purpose.

Sound like anyone you know? I didn't think so. That's because this Perfect Object Woman is a ridiculous, impossible ideal. But that doesn't mean we don't try to become her. The POW is a woman in pursuit of the ideal. She is hostage to an enormous and destructive lie that drives her to excessive behaviors. I can offer a perfect example of this POW pursuit from my own life.

When I was thirty years old, I had a toddler at home, was pregnant with my second child, and attended graduate school full time. Big surprise: I suffered from lots of headaches. But I didn't want to take even an aspirin for my headaches because I thought it would be bad for the baby I was carrying.

One day during a prenatal visit, my obstetrician looked me in the eye and asked, "So, Toni, are you planning on lying down for the birth—or will you work your way through that, too?"

That got my attention, and I decided to slow down somewhat during the end of my second pregnancy. But I didn't abandon the superwoman impulse entirely. The habit of doing too much is the object of one of my continuing battles with myself, and one that I share with countless women. I call it overfunctioning. We tend to try to do just too darn much, till we crash from the exhaustion, resentment, or worse. Why do we do it? Because we have internalized the demands of the Object

Culture. We believe we should always be perfect women—beautiful, caring, energetic, and successful—and if we aren't, then something is wrong with us.

Everywhere a woman turns, it seems, society is telling her that to be happy she must trade her individuality for conformity to very narrow definitions of beauty, status, and appropriate behavior. In the U.S. of G., the lies, myths, and stereotypes are torturously contradictory. Women are supposed to be sexy and pure, strong and vulnerable, independent and dependent, *all at the same time!*

The demands made of women don't end with all the prescriptions for how we *should* be. They continue with a long list of prohibitions. According to conventional wisdom, all women must struggle fiercely to avoid the following negative female traits:

Moody	Petty	Childish	Irresponsibile
Passive	Bitchy	Flighty	Inconsistent
Illogical	Demanding	Weak	Jealous

This is only a partial list of the negative attributes many people associate with being female. One that bothers me a lot is the suggestion, heard everywhere, that women who are successful in high-pressure careers are invariably "bitches" seeking to castrate men. "Bitch" is one of OPO's favorite Thinglish words. The term is often used to put down women who have the nerve to speak their minds about any subject. It's a label every woman dreads, and it is used to enforce silence.

Bad as they are, the negative words that describe women are often joined by a list of positive traits— qualities we are supposed to aspire to—that are just as limiting if we let them define us in a rigid way. They include these attributes:

Nurturing	Beautiful	Positive	Enthusiastic
Generous	Lively	Selfless	Patient
Humble	Caregiving	Agreeable	Sexy

All of these traits are deemed admirable, even neces- sary, for women. Put together, they yield a generic, ever-pleasing personality. This personality is the glossy exterior we present to others, as if it's a fancy brochure. A woman with a "good" personality, according to the generic standard, is always charming, funny, caring, and cheerful. In short, she is "nice."

Of course, being nice is a rather bland choice. As a friend of mine says, "It's like wearing beige and smiling." However, a woman with a "nice" personality may feel safe from harsh judgments, even if she is a little bored and boring.

Personality is, by the way, a poor substitute for the Real essence of a woman, which can be found in her character. Character is represented by core values. A person of good character has integrity. She is a strong and honest individual. She doesn't sacrifice her values in order to present a pleasing personality to the world. Fortunately, all of us have the makings of good character. It is the part that makes us desire to be Real. It is the part that feels bad when we pretend to be someone we are not. If you ignore it long enough, it will demand that you stop playing roles and start becoming yourself.

The Perfect Object Woman combines a nice personality with a beautiful and sexy physical self in order to become a sure success. The value of superficial beauty is confirmed as couples pair up in adulthood. The woman who is devoted to the POW ideal is more likely to get the high-status partner. A woman who has Real talent, Real intelligence, Real skill, or Real achievements, but falls short of society's standards for sex appeal, may be out of luck entirely. So we frantically eroticize ourselves, buying the latest curve-enhancing bras and slipping into garments that may be uncomfortable but communicate that we are sexy and young.

Have you ever considered the difference between underwear options for men and women? For men, the options are boxers or briefs. For women, it's shapewear, bikini, thong, briefs, high or low cut, pantyhose, underwire, demicup, push-up, padded, or minimizing.

And underwear is just the beginning of the vastly more complicated process women endure just to be presentable. After lingerie, a woman must don her makeup—primer, foundation, blush, powder, eye shadow, eyebrow pencil, mascara, lip liner, lipstick, gloss, perfume. Next she carefully picks out her clothes and then her shoes, which often hurt!

Women who have trouble making all the right fashion and makeup moves are aided (or confused) by an enormous beauty-related media industry that tells us "What to Wear Now!" Every day, week, month, the rules change just a little, which means we have to keep buying the magazines and tuning into the TV shows, or we run the risk of being shamefully out-of-date.

If, after all the trying, a woman isn't happy with the image in the mirror, a severe diet, driven by self-loathing, can become part of her routine. I recently read of a gifted writer who starved herself so she could wear jeans that were cut low to reveal her stomach. The diet worked for a while, but then nature brought back her round tummy. She resented the tyranny of fashion and understood what it was doing to her, but she remained so ashamed of herself that she sucked in her stomach when she was in public. (What could this writer accomplish, I wonder, if she didn't put so much thought and effort into her stomach?)

Ironically, even if the writer had kept her belly flat, she wouldn't have been a POW for long. This is because the beauty ideal changes with every shopping season. "What's Sexy NOW!" screams the magazine cover, signaling a shift that will make us feel ugly again and send us running to the store or the plastic surgeon. If you are caught up in the never-ending pursuit of being a POW, don't blame yourself. I have been studying the effects of culture on women for decades, and I know the power of the Object Culture and OPO. I also recognize that women are disempowered by all this focus on physical appearance. It makes us insecure and detracts us from other important aspects of life. Yet like most women I know, I struggle every day to strike the proper balance between reasonable self-care and obsessing over looking perfect according to generic standards. I own, I suspect, more than my share of lotions and potions to stave off the signs of aging. Sometimes I catch myself devoting too much time and too much energy to this effort at the expense of my own Real interests and peace of mind. When this happens I have to recover my balance, making sure that I choose to be beautiful in my own way.

It helps me to remember that while the Object Culture promises the world belongs to the POWs, this is never true. This is obvious when you consider the travails of the young, thin, sexy, and famous pop stars who seem never able to find sustaining relationships and true happiness. But it's also obvious among the so-called sexy women we all know. The joyless face of a "successful" woman in the mall, perusing the latest styles, tells you there's something missing in her life. She's succumbed to the influence of a culture that pressures her to conform to standards that are unnatural, abnormal, and impossible to maintain. In a bit of reverse snobbery, we may snidely refer to her as a "fashion victim." A kinder, more empathetic point of view would consider that most of these POWs are desperately *hungry*, both physically and emotionally.

At its very worst, the POW pursuit leads to self-hatred and severe emotional problems. One of the most obvious is the category of behaviors called eating disorders—

abusive fasting, gorging, purging—which afflicts millions of women and just a handful of men. Patients I have treated for eating disorders tend to be those who try the hardest to be perfect and, on some level, feel tyrannized by this pursuit. By not eating, or by practicing some other destructive behavior, these women claim one aspect of their lives where they exercise total and perfect control. Nothing anyone does can take that control away from them. One eating-disordered patient even told me that while she loves her newborn son and prayerfully promises him to "always be there," she worries that her anorexia may one day take her away from him.

A Woman's Reality Crisis

et's say you're with me so far—you can see the ways we are all pressured to define ourselves according to the unfair myths, stereotypes, and standards of the Object Culture. Do you find yourself responding to OPO almost reflexively, with a constant all-out effort to identify with the positive qualities of conventionally beautiful and successful women and to reject anything that might lead people to label you with the negative ones? You may have realized that the effort you put out and the price you pay are enormous. In your effort to present to the world a false but always cheerful personality, you can wind up smothering your true self. The longer this goes on, the more weary and frustrated you will feel until you reach a point that can only be called a Reality Crisis.

The Reality Crisis is a moment of anguish when you realize you have sacrificed too much for an unworthy ideal. Generally beginning as a mixture of anxiety, fear, anger, depression, and frustration, a Reality Crisis happens when you realize that you have made yourself as perfect as you're ever going to get, and it's still not enough. Worse, you can see for the first time that you have given away too much of yourself—your time, your strength, your heart—in this impossible quest.

When women come into my office and say with a deep sigh that they are suffering from "too much stress," I've found this to be a Reality Crisis signal. As we talk about this feeling of stress, these women begin to understand their feelings are not as much a response to demands on their time as they are a sign that they are overwhelmed by the feelings of shame and guilt that come when we don't satisfy the demands, the *shoulds*, that OPO is shouting in our ears. A woman will not report she feels stress when she is deeply engaged in a life she has designed herself and loves.

Facing a Reality Crisis, women feel stressed-out because they are trying desperately to live up to some culturally defined *shoulds* and feel guilty because they are failing. They think they should be POWs but know they aren't hacking it. For these women who are punishing themselves because they have internalized OPO, I redefine stress to mean:

Self-applied
Torture in
Response to
Extreme
Should
Situations

Coming into therapy, women may label their stress as the result of a relationship crisis, addiction, depression, anxiety attacks, or some other big problem, but beneath that sense of stress, women hide anger, resentment, frustration, and even grief related to the loss of their Real selves.

One client of mine had tried to erase her Real self

and become a woman she and I playfully dubbed "Betty Bland." Dreadfully afraid of being judged a bitch, Betty tried to make herself acceptable to everyone. She never said anything controversial, never complained, never spoke up. But the silence never felt comfortable to her. She was, she said, "like a loaf of tasteless store brand white bread" who dreamed of being, instead, a loaf of "crusty, spicy, fresh-from-the-bakery-oven Italian garlic bread."

The sense of loss she felt when she realized she had made herself into tasteless, spongy white bread was so painful and profound that it was hard for Betty to express. In her case, and others, we create art to get around the blockage. I asked her to draw a picture based on her feelings that showed herself in the world. It's a very useful exercise that you can try yourself.

Draw Your Pain

Take a sheet of paper and some markers or crayons and make a picture that represents how you feel as you navigate through life. Don't worry about composition, color, or technique. Just let go and draw how you feel.

What have you drawn? What does it say to you?

One of the most poignant results of this exercise I ever saw was a blank sheet of paper marked with a tiny, pale, perfectly round pink dot. The woman who drew this self-portrait explained that she had sacrificed everything so that no one would consider her needy, imposing, selfish, or demanding. In short, she had made herself so small and insignificant that she was almost invisible.

In other cases, women draw dark images that symbolize the hurt they have felt as they destroyed various parts of their personalities. One woman I worked with drew an image of quicksand—she called it "the murk"—and talked about how it swallowed up many different pieces of her.

With the mask exercise (explained in Velveteen Principle #1), many women discover that they have gradually stopped investing time and energy in activities and interests that they once valued. Valuable parts of themselves have been lost. Losses like these can make us feel both grief and anger, and these emotions can bubble up in surprising ways. I think that they are present and influence us when we make cutting remarks to others or have a hostile attitude that seems to arise out of nowhere. Recognizing this kind of behavior in yourself can be terribly unsettling, even if you know that it is caused by the losses you have experienced over a lifetime. That's when we wonder if we really *are* bitches. We aren't, by the way. We are, instead, just women living in the U.S. of G.

Fortunately, a Reality Crisis offers us more than pain and frustration. It gives us a chance to make different choices. We don't have to believe everything our parents, partners, husbands, children, and friends tell us. We don't have to listen to the television or heed the headlines in the magazine that promise "A More Perfect You!" Instead, we can start asserting ourselves with the most basic tool we can use to become Real— the Beliefs–Feelings–Behaviors formula.

Real Beliefs, Feelings, and Behaviors

How we feel about ourselves, our work, our relationships, our lives depends entirely on our beliefs. How are these beliefs developed? They are acquired in a variety of ways. As children we get our beliefs from adults who teach us that we will be rewarded for compliance and punished for disobedience. When we are grown, the wider world takes over this job. We play office politics and receive a raise in pay. We dress seductively and get attention. We strive for the generic ideal, and learn how to reduce the gossip, abuse, and judgment—OPO—that people heap on nonconformists.

Women who accept the perfection myth believe with all their hearts that they must have a perfect home, the best children, and the ideal husband. Their *belief*—that they must achieve perfection—guarantees that they will *feel* unhappy, dissatisfied, and worse. These feelings will lead to *behaviors*—more striving and struggling and self-criticism—that only make matters worse.

Those behaviors make things worse for everyone around you, too. If we believe in perfection, then we may expect perfection from other people—friends, family, partners—and push them to meet our expectations. A woman who believes she must maintain the perfect home, for example, has every reason in the world to expect consistent cooperation from everyone else who lives there. This is exactly what happened in the family of two children I have seen for counseling. They are literally terrorized by their mother's anxious approach to homemaking. She's so nervous about OPO that she and her husband and children have long "to do" lists every weekend. She gets a clean, well-maintained home, but her family dreads Saturdays and resents her all week long. Because of her belief system, her focus is on her home, and she scarcely makes time available for her children or herself as Real people.

What if this mother stopped believing in the race to be perfect and just dropped out of the competition? For one thing she would *feel* a whole lot more relaxed. She would also *behave* differently toward her children. No doubt, some of that time she once devoted to weekend cleaning would be used to connect with her Real self and the people in her family in a more positive and happy way.

The effects of a change in belief can ripple out in many ways. If that supercleaning mom chose to value relationships more, she and her children would feel better about themselves. They would feel more connected and gradually become more open, relaxed, and committed to their own interests and passions. In short, they would be more Real.

The same process can begin for you if you just examine your beliefs and start making adjustments. Wouldn't you express yourself more openly, engage in life more fully, if you stopped being afraid that your clothes, your skin, and your home were ugly or defective, or that your main purpose in life is to satisfy the expectations of those around you? How much have you given up? How many times have you not spoken up because you were afraid you didn't measure up to some superficial standard? How many of life's rewards have you lost because you believe you are not smart enough, not important enough, or otherwise not worthy?

What if you developed *your own* set of beliefs that defined your purpose in life and allowed yourself to be guided by them instead? The possibilities are almost dizzying. You could believe . . .

you are beautiful just the way you are.
you already have enough stuff.

you have a right to speak up.
your creative energies deserve an outlet.
you are worthy of love and respect.
no one else can define you.

These are the types of beliefs we can adopt as a start-ing point on the road to being Real. But they are only examples. In the Real world, there are no one-size-fits-all solutions. Every one of us is born with the right to set aside the strict dictates of the Object Culture, to dis-cover what we believe, and to live according to those beliefs. Of course, we are bound by laws and physical limits. (I won't ever be a champion figure skater no matter how much I believe I could be.) But beyond these limits lies a truly exciting range of possibilities.

To be Real is to be your complete, whole, idiosyn-cratic self. It is our purpose in life, and when women understand that it's possible, they can feel both excited and eager about their own potential. At one talk I gave to discus this idea, a young woman expressed these feelings directly, asking in a near-whisper, "How do I start?"

I believe you must start by recognizing that so many of the problems you experience are caused by merely liv-ing in an Object Culture, which perpetuates destructive myths about women and demands we deny our individuality and conform to a single prescription for happiness. This explains why so many of us are constantly tired, anxious, and downhearted. Denying who you are is exhausting and dispiriting. It also explains why we seek psychotherapy twice as often as men, and it is why 90 percent of the visitors to the Velveteen Principles website are female. Together their comments and stories reveal feelings of anguish, frustration, and a deep desire to revolt against the impossible, soul-chilling standards of the Object Culture.

If we understand the forces allied against our Real selves and have some basic principles for fighting against them, we can, one by one, wage a sort of Velveteen Revolution. This revolution would transform us with a different, more Realistic set of standards, values, and practices. We can create a new vocabulary of success, and pursue happiness and fulfillment as we define them. We can each make a declaration—I'm Real, and I'm not going to fake it anymore!—that women can rally around.

The Velveteen Principles for Women is written for the girl photographed on that boulder and every other girl who was taught to strive for an impossible ideal and thereby came to doubt herself when she fell short. I intend this book to serve as both an inspiration and a source of techniques and values that can be adopted in whatever measure you choose. Some of you may find yourself focusing on the sections about courage. Others might be more partial to the principles of gratitude and honesty. But for every one of us, the starting point is to know that it is possible to be a Real woman.

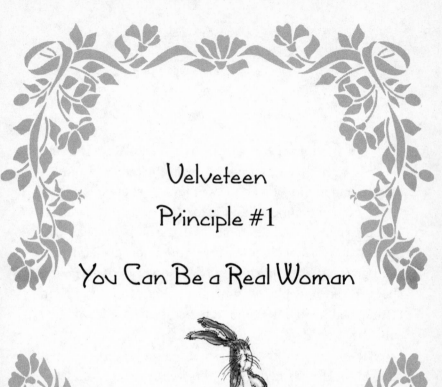

Velveteen

Principle #1

You Can Be a Real Woman

In the nursery where the Velveteen Rabbit lived, the high-status toys buzzed, clicked, and moved under the power of windup mechanisms. They bragged and competed and made fun of the little bunny. Alone among the inhabitants of the nursery was one who had seen mechanical toys come and go, and who had grown worn and shabby but also very wise. Having been loved and played with for a long time, the Skin Horse had lost all his fur and most of his tail, but he had also become Real.

The process of becoming real would be difficult, but the Skin Horse made sure the bunny understood the reward: a life of love, acceptance, and self-assurance. The Rabbit was convinced. Even though the Skin Horse said the journey could be long and painful, the bunny "longed to become Real, to know what it felt like," writes Margery Williams.

The Velveteen Rabbit was fortunate. He found a mentor and exemplar, someone whose very life proved that it was possible to become Real. The Skin Horse would be his inspiration and his guide, and the Rabbit would move rather steadily toward becoming Real.

For women who want to make the same journey, it can be hard to find a Skin Horse to guide them. It can be a struggle to even hold on to the dream of becoming Real and resist falling back into the habits of a Perfect Object Woman. The key is to fight the numbed-out feeling we all get from overexposure to the Object Culture—media, materialism, competition—and stay fully conscious of our feelings and experiences. Our minds can either enslave us or save us. If we hope to be Real, we have to first understand our starting point.

Every woman who makes the decision to be fully conscious and become Real immediately comes face-to-face with the compromise, accommodation, and denial she once used as she tried to make it in the United States of Generica. All of us have done this, presenting ourselves to the world as if we are perfect. Living "as if" involves more than a little denial and self-deception. To keep this in mind, I use the letters of those two words—AS IF—to explain the process. When we live AS IF, we are . . .

Absent. We blankly accept the standards of OPO (Other People's Opinions) and tune out our individuality.

Superficial. We judge ourselves on outward appearances, and our financial and social statuses.

Insecure. We feel so much anxiety that we try to control ourselves and others by never being spontaneous.

Fearful. We are so afraid of OPO and failing to succeed as POWs that we are terrified to admit our own imperfections.

No one who lives AS IF can be happy. It is a self-deluding way of living, and it robs us, and the people we care about, of authentic experiences. It can be very painful to discover you are an AS IF woman. But we cannot choose a different way without acknowledging this truth. This is never easy because we often feel ashamed about neglecting our true selves and because OPO is always there speaking Thinglish, the language of the Object Culture, trying to drag us back.

Gerry, a forty-year-old woman I have treated in my psychotherapy practice, decided she would try to become Real after ending a relationship with yet another abusive partner, her third in ten years. She went back to school, enrolling at a local college and, in our sessions together, began facing her chronic low self-esteem, which had plagued her for many years.

Believing she was not pretty or impressive enough to deserve more, "I always settled for the best loser in the bar," Gerry explained with an ironic chuckle. When these men turned out to be mean, angry, and even violent, a part of Gerry thought that she was having these terrible relationships because she wasn't a successful POW.

Admitting how she had let herself become trapped by her negative self-image was painful for Gerry. These kinds of realizations sometimes made her angry at herself, and she said, "My God, how could I have been so stupid?" It helped her to know that she had been under the influence of the Object Culture and OPO. Even the self-criticism she voiced in my office—calling herself stupid, for example—came from OPO, which she had internalized. At times like this, when she saw how she was surrounded by negative messages that made her question her own value, Gerry would ask out loud, "How is it even possible for someone to become Real? How do you even start?"

Handwritten margin notes (top left):

(OBD)

Outside:
Financially well off, great instructor(s), clean nice house, children, into are perfect, college educated, perfect mate, life

Discover Yourself

appily, by the time any woman asks, "How can I become Real?" she has already begun to trade an AS IF life for a Real one. The simple act of considering the conflict between our true inner values and the false front we present to the world puts us on the path to being Real. Fortunately, we can use a few tools to move along a bit faster. One is a classic art therapy exercise called the mask. Gerry undertook this exercise on her own between visits to my office. It is designed to help us recognize the false selves we've adopted to satisfy OPO and the Real selves we long to be.

The Mask

The mask exercise can be done using a variety of materials. The simplest masks are made with a sheet of paper and some crayons or markers. More complex masks can be made with cloth or, if you know how, with papier-mâché or other sculpting materials.

Handwritten margin notes (bottom):

I am 1/2 way there, but tend to fall back into the Object Culture.

Using words, drawings, and images cut out of magazines, photos, and anything else you desire, decorate the side of the mask that is turned out for others to see when you wear it. This side represents the image you have always tried to present as you strove to be a POW.

Once the outside is done, repeat the process on the *inside* of the mask, the part that lies against your face. This time, however, you must choose words, pictures, colors, and other items that represent the inner you, the Real you.

The more time, thought, and feeling you put into making your mask—both sides—the more you will learn about your ongoing struggle with the demands of the Object Culture and the qualities, hopes, dreams, and values you have kept secret from others and, perhaps, from yourself.

When Gerry and I first discussed the mask exercise, she was a little reluctant. "I'm not an artist," she said. I knew OPO was whispering in her ears.

OPO: *This is ridiculous. What a bunch of psychobabble nonsense.*

I was relieved when, after a little argument with herself, Gerry bravely agreed to give the mask exercise a try. The next week, instead of bringing it in, she said that she had made one simple mask with a sheet of paper and markers, and was inspired to do more. She went on the Internet, learned how to make a papier-mâché mask that would be shaped like her own face, and then started surfing for images. "I don't know why," she told me excitedly, "but I'm really into this."

Another two weeks passed before Gerry brought her mask to my office. It was breathtaking. On the outside, which was base coated with a flawless flesh tone, were about a dozen items decoupaged onto the surface. A picture of a blankly smiling fashion model was plastered on one cheek. A piece of a dollar bill was stuck to the chin. The words *running on empty* ran along her jaw line. On the forehead was pasted a picture of Mr. Clean, and next to that was a picture of a push-up bra carefully snipped out of a catalog.

The inside of Gerry's mask, the part no one could see because it was pressed against her face, was base coated in fierce-looking tiger stripes. She had drawn a tall pine tree right up the center of the mask, from chin to forehead, to represent her love of nature. Among the items lacquered to the surface were a photo of her as a girl receiving a diploma, a picture of a motorcycle, a pair of hands pressed together in prayer, and a panel from an old Peanuts cartoon showing Lucy offering psychotherapy for five cents.

What did the mask reveal about Gerry? The outside showed how hard she had struggled to conform to the POW ideal and how it had left her feeling empty. The inside revealed passions, hopes, and dreams she had always felt. Gerry loved travel, nature, and education, and she was thinking about doing some kind of work that involved helping others. She also longed to have time for meditation and yoga, two spiritually enriching practices she had abandoned because she was too busy for them.

The nature of the two sides of the mask didn't shock Gerry. A part of her had always known that she had neglected big parts of herself in order to adapt to the demands of the world. But creating the mask had allowed her to touch and feel this conflict in a new way. And for as long as I worked with her, she kept it on display in her home, where it inspired her to continue her education, travel, and, eventually, pursue both a new career in social work and, even better, more positive relationships.

Hallmarks of a Real Woman

Gerry made her shift from aspiring POW to Real woman in a slow and steady way. She didn't make any rash and radical moves, and she always understood that she would have to make certain compromises with the Object Culture. Unless and until there's a social revolution of some sort, the Object Culture is here to stay, and we must understand that life requires certain compromises with it. For example, you are not going to succeed in a formal office setting, or even keep your job, if you refuse to dress according to the workplace culture. Indeed, for practical reasons we must all look like generic women from time to time, and there is no reason to refuse to play this or any other necessary role. Nor should we judge ourselves, or others, for doing so.

The difference for those who live as Real women can be seen in the way they think about these roles and balance the things they must do to satisfy certain conventions with idiosyncratic expressions of their Real values. You cannot change the Object Culture on your own, but you do have complete control over your response to it. That is your power, and it is a formidable thing.

What are the hallmarks of being a Real woman? Women who are Real believe their happiness depends on following their own passions and definitions for success. They have taken the time to identify their own needs and priorities, and rather than focusing exclusively on the approval of others, they organize their lives so that some of their time and energy is spent on themselves. I'm not talking about sitting around eating bonbons and flipping through magazines, although there's nothing wrong with that once in a while. I'm referring instead to crafting a life that is satisfying and true to your own heart and mind.

Certainly there are great women of history who fit the definition of Real. My Real Women Hall of Fame is filled with the likes of Harriet Tubman, Sandra Day O'Connor, Rachel Carson, Althea Gibson, and hundreds more who followed their passions, defined their own lives, and made great marks. One of my all-time favorite Real women was Julia Child. Almost fifty when her first cookbook was published, she turned her passion for food into a joyous career. Although her cooking was first-rate, it was Julia's generosity and lack of inhibition, evident on her TV shows, that made her well loved.

But you don't have to be great or do conspicuously great things to be Real. Nor do you have to be an outspoken rebel or a suffering artist. Women become Real when they examine and select their own beliefs, honor their own values and passions, and accept themselves as they are.

Once you know what to look for, you start to see Real women wherever you go. I recently found several of them about twenty miles from my house, at the end of a long dirt road that follows a little-used railroad line. These women own and run the most unusual nursery and garden center I have ever seen. The place is a rustic wonderland of gardens, trees, and endless rows of potted plants. The floras are arranged according to certain themes, with pathways cut so you can experience everything from tropical species to bonsai.

However, the most important living and growing organisms in the nursery were the women who dig, prune, sweat, and feed the plants. They wear comfortable work clothes and very little makeup. Some have their hair cropped short. Others tie their hair back, accepting the inevitable wisps and tangles. They get dirty and tired. But when you ask a question about a specific plant, they respond with remarkable passion. Yes, they know the right growing conditions for that hydrangea. No, they don't have those particular bulbs in stock, but they would be happy to order them.

Happiness seemed to reside in every corner of that nursery because it is more than a business. It is a product and reflection of the passions and personalities of the women who own and run it. They are so committed to their interest that they won't waste time or energy, which would be better spent in the nursery, on striving for the generic ideal. Perfect nails, clothes, makeup, and social skills are beside the point—and not very useful. These women possess something much better: Real lives engaged in a Real passion in a very Real place.

Of course, you don't have to find a dozen acres of land and create a gardener's paradise—or achieve some other grand goal—to be Real. We are Real when we stop being ruled by shoulds and Other People's Opinions and express ourselves freely. We are Real whenever we immerse ourselves in something we truly love. My daughter is Real when she sits at the piano and loses herself in composing music. I am Real when I let myself tackle a complex art project—for example, adding a mosaic to a plain, old end table—and give my all to the process.

Good Is Pretty Good

An old expression advises "Perfect is the enemy of good." Some people take this to mean that if they pursue absolute perfection, they won't have to settle for something that is just "good enough." This interpretation misses the point. Although it's hard to find support for this idea in a world that celebrates only those who occupy the peaks of the highest mountains, I would argue that "good" is a very worthy goal. Doesn't it sound good to be a good person who does good work, has good relationships, and feels good about your life?

The pursuit of perfection, on the other hand, can be a path to frustration, anxiety, and exhaustion. You may recall that in the nursery where Margery Williams's Velveteen Rabbit lived, the shiny mechanical toys that seemed perfect tended to break easily. I think the same is true for people. When we reach for perfection, we set an impossible goal. As we strain to reach it, we become not strong but brittle because we lose the individuality and perspective that makes women both stable and flexible.

This is not to say that you shouldn't do your best. Of course you should. But no one performs at peak levels all the time. Every artist makes mistakes. Every champion loses. Only those who understand that mistakes and losses are inevitable in life have the inner strength to carry on. In fact, most setbacks are really just opportunities to grow and develop. The key is to avoid feeling so ashamed of your setbacks that you deny what is happening or feel immobilized by self-criticism.

OPO's most powerful weapon, shame, makes us feel as if we have broken some very important social rules and risk losing our connection with others. Human beings are social animals. We need a community to survive. Shame threatens us with isolation. The fear of banishment—because we are flawed, opinionated, or otherwise different—is a powerful obstacle to becoming Real. But the truth is that most of the shame that people feel is entirely unreasonable. We must fight against hating ourselves because we are imperfect and instead accept our flaws. If we do this, we can actually learn from our mistakes.

This is, admittedly, easier said than done, especially when we consider all the ways we are pressured, by other people and the mass media, to chase perfection. The perfection ideology is very good for business. It makes people feel insecure and drives them to buy the newest running shoe, the latest diet supplement, and the most advanced computer. When TV ads and magazines tell us about the new best restaurant or resort, these places are overwhelmed by requests for reservations. This is because so many of us are uncertain about our own judgment and are so concerned about making mistakes that we would rather let the experts in business and the media tell us what to do.

The Real women I know refuse to be trapped in the pursuit of perfection. Instead they maximize the times when they can be their Real selves and try to hold on to their perspective even when they are forced to play certain roles. In either situation, these women are Real because their actions are based on free and self-defined deliberate choices.

Besides committing to their own values, Real women make peace with who they are. They accept in their hearts and minds that they are never going to be perfect according to the Object Culture's definitions. If you want to do this, it helps to accept every part of yourself, even the ones that OPO doesn't like. I, for example, have always heard that I am "intense." For a while I resisted this characterization. POWs are supposed to be relaxed, easygoing, and coolheaded. Sorry, that's not me. I'm a very tuned-in, analytical, and alert woman. There's no shame in this truth, and if I'm going to be Real, I have to accept it.

On a more superficial level, I must also accept my thighs. They are never going to be tight and muscled like the ones I see on TV. Should I be stoned and mocked because of this? Or should I be allowed to be happy and loved? I choose to embrace my saggy, cellulite-riddled, pasty-white legs. They've taken me everywhere I've gone in my life, and I appreciate their loyalty.

Perhaps the best response every woman can make when confronted with her so-called flaws involves asking a simple question—So what?

The So What? Dialogue

Most of us forget to test the validity of our worries and self-criticism. We *feel* bad about ourselves or a particular issue and assume we're correct to be troubled. A flaw or a mistake seems like a serious problem.

Very few things in life present us with genuinely profound and disturbing consequences. More commonly, we scare ourselves when it's hardly necessary. The next time you find yourself judging yourself harshly, start asking the magic question—So what?—and keep asking and answering until you discover a new point of view.

How does this work? Take, for example, my concern about jiggly thighs. The So what? dialogue might sound like this:

Oh, no, I have really jiggly thighs.
So what?
So, they don't look like they are supposed to.
So what?
Well, some people could think I'm ugly.

So what?

Then they might not like me.

So what?

Well . . . I guess nothing. If they don't like me because toned thighs are a high priority, then I guess I'm not missing much.

See how effective this is? In a few short moments, I went from self-criticism to a new perspective. The same thing can happen for you whether you criticize yourself because you can't cook, you aren't rich, you have physical flaws, or for anything else.

With the So what? dialogue, you can see that the only thing you lose when you don't measure up to the standards set for the POW is someone else's approval. And how valuable is that? It is nothing compared with the sense of integrity, self-esteem, and happiness you feel when you know you are a pretty good Real woman. Best of all, that feeling doesn't go away as you age. It can't be taken from you if you lose your job. And it grows deeper and stronger as time passes.

It is a kind of poetic justice that the very society and culture that conspire to make women conform to generic ideals also benefits enormously when we become Real. Real women can contribute far more to others than unReal women can. They can innovate, invent, and create in ways that those who are enslaved by the Object Culture cannot. In the end, naturally enough, Real women add to the richness of relationships, families, and communities in ways that generic women cannot. The Object Culture may not encourage the development of Real women, but humanity needs us, and the world suffers when we neglect our gifts and passions in the fruitless pursuit of generic perfection.

Don't Fear Jumping into the Deep End

When you are Real, make your own choices in life, and follow them to places unknown, it's a lot like jumping into the deep end of a pool. You may be a very good swimmer, but the depths are always a little unsettling.

This is especially true, I believe, for women. We have certain vulnerabilities that demand we muster even more courage than men to strike out on our own.

Difficult as it may be to talk about, all women feel vulnerable at one time or another. In the adult world, we are responsible for our own safety, financial security, and both physical and mental health. In general, it's a little bit harder for women to take care of themselves. We are still paid less in the workplace and therefore have to work harder to be financially independent. But this problem is nowhere near as obvious as the challenge women face when it comes to basic physical safety. We are not as safe as men when we are in strange places or with people we don't know. The problem is even worse for those of us who have been abused physically, sexually, or emotionally. I witnessed the powerful, objectifying force of abuse while working at a community clinic where I counseled many women who had been subjected to both chronic abuse and crimes such as rape. More than a few blamed themselves for what had happened, and some expressed more empathy for the people who had hurt them than for themselves.

Unfortunately, about one-third of all women—including me—have been abused. Abuse teaches a child that she is an Object, a thing to be exploited by another for emotional or physical gratification. Abuse can make us angry, numb, anxious, fearful—you name it. In my psychotherapy practice, I have worked with many women who carry the extra burden of abuse, and I have seen how it can also induce a kind of shame that drives a woman to seek protection in perfection. It disconnects a child from her Real self and leads to an overwhelming sense of insecurity. In fact, I would argue that women who have been victimized are more likely to play out Object Culture roles—perfect daughter, perfect partner, perfect mother—because such roles promise safety and acceptance. Because they are so desperate to be safe and their sense of worth has been damaged, victimized women play roles that don't fit them because they think it's the safe way to be. And they suffer even more when their Reality Crisis hits because they see how much time and energy has been wasted on this unachievable goal. They realize that bending to someone else's values and struggling to fit into the POW mold won't make them feel safe. Instead, it keeps them from developing their own strengths, and they will never be safe and secure until they feel strong inside.

After I was sexually abused as a child, I tried to make

myself invisible. I thought of myself as a dead girl. As a teenager I was depressed, withdrawn, and sarcastic. Later in life I tried to win attention and admiration in the theater and television, even though my secret interest was in psychology. With others I was always wary, afraid to be seen as less than perfect. But in time the pain I felt while playing roles and denying my true self grew so severe that I had to confront it.

During my Reality Crisis, I began psychotherapy to face up to what had happened to me, and I let myself reimagine life. Perhaps the most exciting thing I discovered at this time was that I was not a dead girl, the spark of individuality still burned inside me, and it was possible to stop role playing and start being myself.

The good news is that Real is possible, even if you have been hurt and even if you are afraid of becoming Real. I've seen it happen many times. Formerly abused women I know have recovered their identities and gone back to school, stopped abusing drugs and/or alcohol, left abusive relationships, taken up new careers, changed relationships, and rekindled creative outlets. I have seen them become artists and teachers and women in love with their lives. They also become examples and inspiration for all women who want to be Real. If they can do it, you can too.

Velveteen

Principle #2

Becoming a Real Woman

Is a Process

I can almost hear what some of you are thinking. You've read this far and have become persuaded of a few things. You've recognized the tyranny of the Object Culture and, no doubt, identified some of the ways you have been affected by it. As women we are under enormous pressure to satisfy others and play certain roles according to rigid generic standards. To name just a few:

Daughter—obedient, quiet, pure, pleasing, dutiful

Wife/partner—supportive, beautiful, chaste, sexy, vivacious, sensitive, devoted, thrifty

Mother—nurturing, patient, kind, moral, strict, flexible, playful

Friend—loyal, empathetic, cheerful, fun

Grandmother—generous, wise, steady, soft, steadfast, encouraging

These stereotypes include positive traits (some are covered in the principles in this book), but they are also very limiting, and they require us to be governed by Other People's Opinions about who we *should* be. Those opinions are voiced over and over as we are brought up to be acceptable members of society. This socialization process creates in us what Freud called the "superego," which can hound us from within like an out-of-control conscience.

The superego's main tool, one it shares with our nemesis OPO, is shame. As defined by the eminent theorist Gershon Kaufman, shame is the intense fear that we are defective, our defects will be exposed, and once exposed, those we love will reject us. When parents use shame, the threat is obvious: A child will be punished or abandoned if she does something wrong. When society shames us, it says, "You will be alone because you *are* something wrong."

What kinds of things will the Object Culture shame us for? This list includes being fat, old, infertile, poor, disabled, lesbian, or ugly, but it is much, much longer. Women today feel ashamed if they have a low-status job, if they are not perfectly groomed and dressed, or if they are "moody" or "selfish." You could make your own list, and it's likely you could find one or two items that strike fear in your heart, fear that you will be exposed as defective and therefore shunned. And, of course, as soon as you make the list, OPO will rear its ugly, predictable head and say something like:

OPO: *Don't be ridiculous. I've never heard any-one try to shame women for these things.*

Toni: *That's just the point. Once you are an adult, and parents no longer chastise you harshly, you're not likely to hear someone say out loud, "You ought to be ashamed." But the messages are still there, all around you, in subtle shades and tones. No one says, "You should be ashamed if you don't drive a new car." But every day advertisers make sure you see that happy women drive new cars. Happy women also dye their hair a certain color, have babies to cuddle, and are fit enough to climb mountains. People in our lives repeat these kinds of ideas. Why don't you go shopping, have a baby, lose weight? No one has to* say *that you should feel shame for not measuring up.*

The price women pay to avoid shame can be high. Catherine, a woman I met through the Velveteen Principles website, wrote me to say she had spent eighteen months in a struggle that cost her many friends, deprived her of pleasures like gardening and knitting, and brought her marriage to the brink of divorce. What brought about this struggle? Her determination to fulfill one of the biggest roles expected of women—having a child. Facing significant fertility problems, Catherine wrote that she endured painful medical procedures and was caught in a cyclone of emotions. To make things worse, she blamed herself for not fulfilling her "duties" by playing the role of sister, daughter, friend, etc.

Such is the power of our socialization under the rules of the U.S. of G. that a woman can feel compelled to pursue having a baby at all costs, sacrifice much of what she values in life, and wind up blaming herself when she doesn't reach this goal. In the end, Catherine understood the pressure she had felt to avoid the shame of being perceived as defective. She chose to think about herself differently, to accept she might never have her own biological child, and to research the adoption option.

The socialization of women through shame is a process that slowly erodes our Real selves. It happens very slowly, through years and years of experience. But fortunately there is another process you can choose to begin now and follow over the rest of your lifetime: the process of becoming Real. The fix is not quick. As the Skin Horse said to the Velveteen Rabbit:

You become. It takes a long time. That's why
it doesn't happen to people who break easily, or
have sharp edges, or have to be carefully kept.

The process of becoming Real begins with a commitment that only you can make. The world is not going to push you toward a Real life. And it would be surprising, indeed, for another person to raise the issue out of the blue and say something like, "Go ahead, define yourself on your own terms, and be happy!" But even if they did, it wouldn't matter because you are the only one who can give yourself permission to do it.

The moment you cross this threshold, you have started to be Real. Notice I didn't say that you are on your way to "becoming" Real. No, I say that you are Real with the very first step you take. In fact, becoming a Real woman does begin with a declaration or decision to reconsider your assumptions about life. But that choice is just the beginning. This is because Realness is not a fixed goal. It is not something you achieve. And it is not something you receive like a diploma or award. Being Real is a process that begins when you recognize that there's something more to you than appearance, status, personality, and the roles you play.

The Trouble with Goals

Have you ever felt a letdown shortly after some big achievement or moment in your life? You get the new job you were seeking, buy that dream house, or publish your first book, and the excitement is followed not by a feeling of contentment, but rather by confusion and doubt. You may not actually ask "Is that all there is?" because that question is likely to spark a harsh reply: What's the matter with you? But still you have that feeling.

The victories in our lives satisfy us only for a moment because the pursuit of goals offers us a very limited version of life's possibilities. You have either reached the goal or you haven't. If you haven't, then you can feel anxious, worried, and inadequate. If you have attained the goal, then you must confront the matter of what to do next. Do you stop and let inertia set in, or do you set another goal and plunge yourself right back into another anxious pursuit?

I experienced this syndrome myself when my first book, *The Velveteen Principles*, was published. I had always wanted to share my ideas with others, and that book was a dream come true. But its publication didn't change anything central in my life. Sure, it brought me into contact with new people and experiences, but the basic focus of my life, which is to be Real, didn't change a bit.

The experience reminded me of a Zen proverb: "Before enlightenment, chop wood, carry water. After enlightenment, chop wood, carry water." This means that the Real business of life is in our day-to-day process— chopping wood and carrying water. Reaching a goal, even the goal of enlightenment, doesn't alter this fact.

Don't get me wrong. Goals and achievements are important. They satisfy our desire to create and discover. But our ambitions can't involve just getting a thing or having an experience. This is why the pursuit of fun hardly ever leads to happiness. Fun occurs in the moment, then it is gone. I was reminded of this by a client, Ellen, who had recently returned from one of many trips abroad. Travel excited her, and she always enjoyed planning and taking her vacations. But soon after her return she realized she was back in an unhappy routine—an unfulfilling workday followed by collapsing at home in front of the TV—and she knew she had to change if she would ever be happy.

Happiness is a by-product of passionate engagement in a life that matters to you. Women who "just want to have fun" but have no deeper interests never find peace and contentment. Those who discover and follow their passions as a way of life do.

Unfortunately, anyone who lives in the United States of Generica is subject to continual messages that life requires the constant pursuit of tangible goals, such as money, material goods, and fun experiences. According to this paradigm, worthwhile people compete to win victories in business, sports, and even relationships. To demonstrate your worth, you must win trophies and power and acquire the right clothes, house, car, body, husband, partner, friends, and children.

A host of Thinglish phrases are repeated ad nauseam to support these ideas. Each phrase harbors a subtext that is negative, destructive, or intended to make you spend money.

- *A woman can never be too rich or too thin.* (The ideal is important, but you never reach it and must keep trying forever.)
- *You've got to dress for success.* (So buy more clothes.)
- *You can have it all.* (If you don't, there's something wrong with you.)
- *She's let herself go.* (So she's now worthless.)
- *Winning is everything.* (If you aren't a winner, you're a loser.)
- *You get what you deserve.* (What you own reflects your value.)
- *Because you're worth it.* (Spend more money on your hair.)
- *She's a perfect ten.* (And if you're not, you should be ashamed.)
- *No pain. No gain.* (Keep trying even if the effort hurts you.)
- *It's better to look good than to feel good.* (This one's too obvious!)

These Thinglish phrases echo throughout the Object Culture like mantras. They resonate with today's women because we are far more likely than our mothers were to compete in the workplace and be responsible for all or part of our family's financial security. As a result, we can find ourselves pursuing wealth, career advancements, and other status markers, believing that such goals will soothe our anxieties and give us security. Unfortunately, it's very difficult to determine when "enough is enough"—and every time we climb higher on the ladder of success, we are confronted by the next rung above us.

An orientation toward goals can also bring us trouble in our personal lives. This truth is plain to see in the way so many women approach marriage. At a very early age, the Object Culture teaches girls about the importance of living out the ultimate Princess Paradigm fantasy: a big, fancy wedding. According to the Object Ideal, you are supposed to get engaged in some ultra-romantic fashion to a man who resembles the little plastic grooms that appear atop wedding cakes. From that moment on, you must invest a huge amount of time, energy, and emotion in creating an event that resembles a Hollywood movie starring you, the princess bride.

The pressure women feel as they pursue the goal of the perfect wedding is so enormous and so widely experienced that the nervous, anxious, crying bride-to-be has become a cliché. This perfect-wedding pressure is, nevertheless, so powerful a force that it has sent several women to see me for counseling. In one case I worked with Angela, a woman who was so desperately invested in the goal of the perfect wedding that she was having panic attacks—numbness, shortness of breath, abdominal pain, lightheadedness—that mimicked cardiac episodes. At night, Angela was literally having nightmares about ruining the day by spilling something on her dress.

The Power of Process

Everyone who cared about Angela and noticed her anxiety responded with what they thought were helpful organizational tips. They suggested that she keep notebooks, use a Day Planner, or create color-coded files. With enough effort and attention, they seemed to say, the wedding would be okay, and she would avoid shame and embarrassment.

In our work together, Angela and I took a different

approach. We started by examining the true nature of a wedding and what might make hers a success. In a very short time she concluded that if, at the end of the wedding day, she was happily married to her fiancé, the wedding would be a success. In fact, even if she fell in a giant puddle on her way to the service and stood before the congregation covered in mud, it wouldn't matter. (The So what? dialogue brought her to this conclusion.)

A muddy wedding dress wouldn't matter because a good marriage, which is a lifelong process, is far more important than achieving the momentary goal of an impressive wedding. Real marriages begin when two people make a commitment to love, live, and grow together. These relationships are built on mutual empathy and the belief that we continue to develop throughout our lives. Every day brings new opportunities to learn, and there is no goal—or end point—we will reach that guarantees we have "made it." There is no "making it," only "living it."

In fact, as we discussed the difference between the goal of a wedding and the process of a marriage, Angela and I noticed that when people placed too much emphasis on the wedding, the marriage often didn't work out. We both knew couples who had gotten married in cyclones of excitement and activity. After lavish honeymoons, they came home to new houses with high mortgages and filled with furniture bought on credit. Unprepared for living together, these couples were separated within months.

As Angela came to realize this difference, her panic attacks stopped. She began to focus more on how much she loved the man who was going to be her husband, and she accepted that she could have a lifetime with him to enjoy. Proof that she had really changed came on the day before the wedding, when the florist called to say that flowers selected to match the bridesmaid's gowns had arrived but were the wrong color. Not only didn't she panic, but Angela was so relaxed she could see that she liked them better than the ones she had originally chosen.

When last I saw Angela, she was happily married. Her wedding was a happy memory recalled in photos. Her marriage, on the other hand, was an ongoing relationship that grew stronger each day. She and her husband were devoted to each other's growth and development and understood that their life together was ever-evolving. They were expecting their first child, and the prospect of change and the new things that come with change made them feel alive.

The power of process will, inevitably, affect Angela and her husband as they rear their children. If you are a mother, you have, no doubt, noticed that there are times when you are so deeply engaged in everyday life with your child—teaching her, caring for her, exploring the world with her—that hours, days, even weeks seem to fly by. You may feel physically tired, and it might be impossible for you to point to a major personal achievement reached during this period. But in the process of practicing kindness and generosity, you experienced Real life—and that (along with fostering the growth of another human being) is an achievement itself.

If you approach life as a process and not a series of goals, you don't have to fear that you will suffer some terrible fate if you fail. This is what Angela felt as she contemplated her wedding day. Indeed, she was so afraid of failure (as it was defined by OPO and the Object Culture) that her body reacted with debilitating symptoms. It was as if her subconscious was demanding she get a better perspective on things. When we are freed from the pressure associated with make-or-break goals, we can simply be ourselves. We perform better and achieve more when we are simply relaxed and being ourselves.

Being ourselves without the oppression of a goal becomes obvious when we look at the issue of women's sexuality. The culture stresses goals, of course, with magazine covers offering advice on how to have "your best orgasm ever." But as most women know, orgasm is elusive. The more you try to "get one," the less likely you are to have a satisfying experience. Real love-making is a process. Orgasm is just one part of it. It's a good part, but only one part. And it generally arrives when you are more concerned with the less goal-oriented aspects of sex, like connectedness and staying present with your partner.

The same dynamic holds true in other areas of life that involve emotions and creativity. In the arts and sports, for example, a commitment to process puts us in a relaxed state of self-assurance called "flow." Its opposite, a high-pressured, anxious approach to life, leads to problems like stage fright, writer's block, and so-called "choking" while on the playing field. When you are in the flow, you don't worry about where you stand on the ladder of achievement. You know that all human beings have an equal right to respect and happiness. And all the achievements, acquisitions, and status in the world won't guarantee you will feel self-worth or have any greater peace of mind.

For single women, approaching life as a process offers liberation from the tyranny of goals set by OPO. When you stop trying so hard to be like everyone else, you suddenly have the time and energy to be Real yourself. Some women are wary of this idea. They tell me they are afraid that as they become Real, other people will reject them. Those who want a relationship even worry that potential partners will be frightened away. Given all the pressure to conform, I know it's hard to believe, but women who allow themselves to become Real individuals actually find that many people are drawn to them.

This can happen, and you can grow ever more Real as long as you are engaged in a positive process. But beware. The loss of what's Real in us and in our lives is a gradual process, too. It is caused by the powerful forces of OPO and the Object Culture. The only way to stave off this erosion is with a vigilant commitment to being Real.

What Do You Believe?

ather than being Real, it seems like it would be easier to accept the Object Culture's message—devote your life to chasing goals—and join the crowd. That way you are excused from the risks associated with developing your own agenda for life based on your own set of beliefs. Also, there is a chance that in the pursuit of certain prizes you will find some satisfaction. But inevitably, the temporary highs that come as we skip from one achievement to another fail to satisfy, and whether or not you yet realize it, like the Velveteen Rabbit, you ache for Realness.

At this moment, when we feel the hunger for something deeper, we have the opportunity to adopt a life-as-process orientation based on our own beliefs. Among other sources, you may draw these core values from your religious faith, classical ethics, literature, and/or wise people you know and love (including yourself). Instead of adopting a concept automatically because it is dictated to you by some source or authority, you can adopt beliefs based on your own experience and analysis. The very best tool to use in this process is a three-letter word that forms a simple question every child likes to repeat as she explores the world—Why?

I Wonder Why

One of the most important lessons I ever learned in graduate school was taught by a professor who seemed to have a sixth sense when it came to analyzing the motivations of individuals and groups. He explained that people tend to claim that they hold one certain set of ideals and goals—he called it the "obvious agenda"—while they often quietly follow another, which he called the "hidden agenda."

In situations where you feel confused about the beliefs people hold (or the beliefs you cling to), the answer can be found by analyzing the situation the same way a child might—by repeatedly asking Why?—to discover the hidden agenda that's in play.

Here are some examples:

Many groups, including businesses, religions, political parties, and even clubs, demand unwavering loyalty. Why?

Families often sacrifice the dreams of individuals for the good of the group. Why?

Single women are constantly asked, "When are you going to get married?" Why?

Childless couples are urged to have children. Why?

Champion athletes are considered heroes. Why?

Children who don't fit in are treated as outcasts. Why?

These are just a few examples of the Object-oriented ideas women commonly store in their inventories of beliefs. As you explore your own belief system, the opportunities to ask why are endless. You will have your own answers. My answers, when it comes to the questions posed above, suggest that society can be intolerant of individuality, that groups are afraid of dissent, and that our culture tends to value only those qualities that can be measured numerically. Everyone is ready to admire the runner who crosses the finish line first and the student who gets the highest score.

It's a bit harder to appreciate things we cannot measure, such as kindness, empathy, sincerity, and integrity. We recognize these traits in ourselves and others, but they are immeasurable.

Answering key questions about our beliefs is not easy. Indeed, one-word questions like Why? can seem like big challenges. For this reason a lot of parents answer their children with impatient nonsense like the cliché "Because I said so." But if you are brave, you can question your own beliefs in a calm and measured way. Honor that sometimes annoying inner child of yours who constantly asks "Why?" If your answers seem inadequate—such as "I believe this because I always have"—then you may want to reconsider your assumptions.

When we try to live according to beliefs that don't quite fit us, we invariably feel uncomfortable. Sometimes it's a small thing. A woman I know was taught that good girls wear dresses, stay clean, and sit quietly, but she prefers jeans and enjoys working as a mechanic, and felt uneasy expressing those parts of herself. When she examined her old assumptions about good girls and formally struck them from her set of beliefs, she was able to ask the important questions, develop her own answers, and commit herself to her pursuits, including motorcycle repair, without nagging doubts and ambivalence.

Many of the beliefs we live by as adults were installed in our hearts and minds when we were children, and we had no choice but to accept them. Some, like the one about girls and dresses, are general. Others are more specific. Another woman I know was criticized as a girl because she liked to be alone. She always felt hurt by this "loner" label, and she forced herself to be outwardly social. Then as an adult, she discovered she simply enjoyed time spent by herself. She changed her beliefs, deciding that solitude was okay, and instantly felt much better about herself.

The process of identifying the beliefs we live by, rejecting some and adopting others, can and should last a lifetime. When you are Real, you constantly learn and grow. New information and new understanding can change your perspective. In your twenties, you may believe the most important thing in your life is freedom. At age sixty, you might rank personal integrity or connectedness higher on the scale. The key is to avoid rigidity. Don't make your beliefs a form of tyranny. Make them a deliberately chosen, value-rich set of guidelines that will help you create a life process that is a unique, never-ending story.

Velveteen

Principle #3

Real Women Are Emotional

hen he was a little more than a year old, Terry brought her son, Adam, to my office. He was a long-awaited and much-appreciated child, and as he toddled between the sofas where his mother and I sat, Adam and Terry beamed at each other. He would gurgle, and she would gurgle back. He would make hesitant steps away from her, then fling himself back into her arms with laughing abandon. He knew she would catch him, and she always did.

For several minutes during their visit, Adam and Terry were so emotionally connected that their touching, vocalizing, and smiles were entirely spontaneous. Looking at their bright eyes, I found it hard to imagine anyone being more authentic in their emotions, or more relaxed. Later when we talked, Terry explained that she felt completely alive, completely Real, caring for her son. When they were together, her feelings were clear and strong, and she knew exactly how to behave.

Feelings, and the ability to recognize them and be guided by them, are vital to being Real. Indeed, Real women understand that emotions are remarkably accurate reminders of our true values and are signals that point us toward a happier, more fulfilling life. Sadly, in the Object Culture, where everyone is supposed to project happiness, confidence, and coolness at all times, emotions are regarded as a liability. This is especially true for women and girls, who are chastised and criticized for having feelings at all.

OPO: *Stop being so emotional. Calm down. You're too intense! Can't you just relax? Can't you be logical and stop being overly sensitive?*

Toni: *That is such tired talk, OPO. What's your point? You don't want to feel, so you are going to shame us into denying our emotions? Emotions have a lot to teach us. They are valuable. The key is how we use them.*

In an Object-oriented society that values goals, measurements, and comparisons, the seemingly ephemeral realm of emotions receives very little respect. Most professions—except perhaps the arts and sometimes health care—seek to eliminate feelings from their practices. And experts advise us against listening to our hearts when making our biggest decisions. It's better to coldly calculate the odds or weigh the pros and cons, we are told.

Besides being devalued as illogical, human emotions suffer from a cultural association with both weakness and immaturity. Children may express their feelings. Grown-ups are supposed to be restrained. Withholding the expression of emotions—so that one might make clearer judgments—is considered a sign of strength. Finally, emotions are associated with negative female stereotypes. Because we are more connected with our feelings, women are judged to be flighty, irrational, and less sensible than men. Together, all these cultural interpretations of emotion exert a lot of influence—call it adult peer pressure—on all of us. This pressure leads many women to hide and disguise their feelings for fear of being regarded as worthless, childish, or immature.

The result of all this anti-emotion propaganda is a great deal of confusion and self-doubt. We become like the Velveteen Rabbit, who, Margery Williams wrote, "was made to feel himself very insignificant and common-place" under the peer pressure in the nursery. Women I work with report that they often reject their own feelings for fear that their emotions will invite criticism. Many of us get so good at suppressing our feelings that we actually lose touch with our emotions. We often don't know what we feel, and we mistake this void for calm detachment. This emptiness actually represents the loss of a vital element that makes up a Real human being.

As we go through our emotionally muted, unReal lives, both pleasant and unpleasant feelings build up. Of course, it's the pain that causes problems. Many women have told me they eventually become afraid of their unexpressed sadness, grief, and anger. These emotions become so powerful that these women feel that if they relax and let any feelings out, they will be transformed into the enormous green comic-book monster the Incredible Hulk, whose fury is dangerous to himself and everyone else.

Women who are afraid of becoming the Hulk often cultivate the Betty Bland exterior we discussed earlier; they hope to prove to themselves and the world that they are calm, cool, and nice. But nothing you do with your outside can change what is inside. This was made clear to me by a client, Rita, who seemed very composed and controlled. Early in our work together, Rita drew a representational picture of herself. The drawing showed the surface of a smoldering, bubbling volcano. "I am the surface tension," she said, "struggling to keep the center held. If I don't hold the center, the rage will destroy every recognizable thing, so that there will be utter anni-hilation. I will destroy everything in my path. I must be restricted for my own good, or else I will destroy. Everything that's good, I will destroy."

Rita is a very kind, intelligent woman. But she was so afraid of responding to her own emotions that she chose, instead, to desperately study the U.S. of G. and act the way OPO seemed to expect her to act. Women who are afraid of emotions tend to act AS IF—Absent, Superficial, Insecure, and Fearful. Of course, the Betty Bland approach can work for only so long. Eventually, our feelings build up until we have to let them out. Sometimes this happens in an angry Hulkish way. More typically, however, women turn their feelings inward in a self-destructive manner.

At its very worst, when we lose touch with our feel-ings, we run the risk of developing serious psychologi-cal problems, including substance abuse, sexual acting out, eating disorders, and other compulsions. Many women who cut and burn themselves do so in order to break the terrible numbness they experience because they have lost touch with their emotions. The same is true for women who take unreasonable risks with their health and safety. In my practice, I have worked with different women who have bought illegal weight-loss drugs over the Internet, gambled away paychecks in hopes of raising money to pay off credit-card debt, or exercised to the point of passing out in hopes of getting a perfect body.

These women take risks because they cannot feel fear and doubt that it should stop them. They, and the rest of us who are ambivalent about our emotions, would do well to consider that nature gave us a complex array of feelings for good reason.

Emotions, which we often feel before we have time to actually think about something, can be uncannily accurate. Haven't you had moments when your feelings, or so-called "woman's intuition," proved accurate? There's more reason to have faith in these emotions than you might imagine.

How Feelings Educate and Motivate

It's 10 P.M., and you are walking down a well-lit avenue. As you approach a spot where the street-light has gone out, you notice a hollow feeling in the pit of your stomach. Before your brain can tell you that the shadows might hide danger, you already feel a little bit afraid. That fear provides the kind of early-warning signal that alerts your senses and just might keep you out of danger.

We all have experienced this kind of little drama, and it shows us the value of our emotions in a very particular way. Scientists have shown that the emotional centers in our brains work faster than the parts that produce reason and logic. Feelings can provide remarkably accurate warnings about physically dangerous situations. They also tell us when certain beliefs, actions or even relationships violate our most important values.

Emotions are so essential to the process of becoming Real that when women ask me, "What can I do to become Real?" I invariably tell them to start tuning in to their feelings. Even if you have worked hard to suppress your emotions, they still whisper to you, hoping to be heard. Often, the ones you can hear in the beginning point to conflicts between your behavior and your Real self.

Consider, for example, the last time you were part of a group; you were eager to contribute, but stifled yourself in order to get along and be a "good girl." Well, OPO and the values of the U.S. of G. do say that "nice" women keep their opinions to themselves. (My own mother used to admonish my childhood enthusiasm with a Victorian saying, "Be sweet and let who will be clever.") But if you felt uneasy in your silence, it's because your Real self wanted to speak out. Maybe you have a lot to contribute—to conversations, projects, relationships—and you are ready to share.

In many cases, feelings of self-doubt or guilt are signals of a conflict between emotions and behaviors. Does excessive shopping, overwork, or too much wine in the evening leave an empty feeling in the pit of your stomach? If you pay close attention to the moments when that feeling is strong, you should be able to connect it to a habit or behavior that conflicts with your inner values.

And how about the people in your life who make you feel bad? Isn't that feeling a sign that something's wrong? The same is true when certain people, activities, even places evoke warm, positive feelings. Joy, self-esteem, contentment, and other positive feelings can point us in the direction of a happy life. I'm not talking about the fleeting highs people feel when they acquire new things or reach certain goals. I'm referring, instead, to the deeper emotional experiences that make us feel good about ourselves over the long term. These are the feelings that can guide us toward Real happiness.

When we look at the power of our feelings and see how they can steer us away from danger and toward a better life, the clichés about hysterical, overly emotional women rarely have merit. Yes, people sometimes over-react to feelings and fail to think things through. No one should do anything to excess based on a feeling. But this doesn't mean that feelings, in and of themselves, are a problem. Instead of labeling women as "oversensitive," I would say that too many of us are not skilled enough at reading and responding productively to our own emotions. We get so tangled up in negative beliefs and the destructive values of the Object Culture that we fail to properly interpret our Real feelings.

If we are disconnected from our feelings, we lose aspects of our emotional intelligence, a highly valuable trait that was given wide public attention when Daniel Goleman wrote a book with the same name. In general terms, emotional intelligence involves self-awareness, proper response to feelings, empathy for others, and skilled communication. Ironically, these qualities help make a person successful in the goal-oriented Object Culture, even as they guide us to a happy, satisfied life governed by our idiosyncratic beliefs and values.

Reading Our Emotional Signals

> OPO: *All these feelings you talk about seem like "airy-fairy" nothings. Feelings change from one minute to the next. Why let them control you?*
>
> Toni: *You can listen to your feelings without letting them control you. If you did learn to do this, you might discover they are quite valuable.*

I witnessed a truly remarkable illustration of how feelings provide reliable—and *insistent*—signals to our Real selves when working with a young woman named Erin. Referred to me by a doctor who found no physical explanation for her complaints, Erin suffered from terrible stomach cramps and nausea. A smart and sensitive woman, she suspected that her tummy problems had something to do with her emotionally abusive boyfriend, John. But because she felt sick when she was *with* him, and sick when she contemplated *leaving* him, it was difficult for her to understand just what her feelings were communicating to her. This is common for women who are struggling to be Real but have yet to change their beliefs about what is important to them.

They feel conflicted about many things.

It took some time and a lot of talking before we were able to sift out Erin's feelings. It turned out that deep inside, Erin harbored the erroneous belief that she wasn't worthy of anything better than what she was getting from John. She also thought that she couldn't make it alone, without a partner in her life (another irrational belief).

Once she examined her beliefs, Erin was able to interpret the signals her feelings were sending. The pain she felt when she was *with* John was a Real signal about something that was destructive and needed to be addressed. The feeling that came when she thought about leaving him was linked to outdated beliefs about her worth as a person. Soon enough, Erin was able to bravely leave that destructive relationship and quickly learned that it was better to confront the fear of being alone than to live with the pain she experienced in the relationship.

Although Erin needed a little help to get out of an emotional jam-up, in most cases we can do this work on our own. It helps to respect what your heart has to say. Sometimes the emotional signals we get point us toward happiness and fulfillment. Usually we are not very confused about these signals. If your spirit soars every time you walk into a museum, then it's a safe bet that art or history makes you happy. The same is true for a horse lover who feels most comfortable in a barn or when holding the reins.

Difficulties are more common when we experience emotions that are vague, or mixed, and include more painful feelings such as anxiety, anger, or fear. We can also be fooled by our emotions. We feel vaguely unhappy, but don't know why. When this happens to me, and I can't chalk it up to a passing mood, I play investigative reporter. I ask myself a series of questions about the moments that led to painful feelings.

Investigate Yourself

Clues about your feelings and their meanings can be found if you know how to look for them. All that's required is a little patience and some gentle questions. The next time you get lost in a troubling, unexplained mood, sit quietly and run through the following questions. Write down your answers, and when you are finished, read through them to find out the truth about your state of mind.

Who was I with when this feeling started?
What was I doing?
Where did this encounter take place? (Was it a comfortable place? If not, why not?)
How did I feel in that moment?
Why did I feel that way?

This last question—Why?—is the most important. The answer may be that I was with someone whose presence made me uncomfortable or that something about the place or what was said and done clashed with my values and beliefs. For example, I don't enjoy conversations in which people compare their possessions or statuses in a not-so-subtle attempt to establish a hierarchy. This kind of talk is ubiquitous and often occurs subtly. Sometimes I don't know that I've been dragged through one of these conversations until it's long over and I've had time to consider why I feel down. Then I realize that I had been exposed to a lot of talk about why something in my life—my house, clothes, car, children, husband, or some other thing—didn't measure up.

Feeling Better by Reassessing Your Beliefs

It can be tempting to end your emotional investigation with the impulse to blame someone else—everyone else—for your suffering. Maybe you have finally understood that you often feel depressed after spending time with a certain friend because she mixes significant amounts of subtle criticism or bragging into your conversations. Perhaps your partner-in-life has a habit of talking about that one insecurity you just can't seem to get over. The obvious solution may be to confront these people, tell them how you feel, and ask for a change.

But consider, for a moment, that there are at least two

sides to every human encounter, and it's much easier to change yourself than to change someone else. In fact, it is impossible to change someone else—that way leads to madness, or at least a lifetime of frustration and feelings of failure. Instead, what if you were able to do something about the way you are affected by others that would provide you with protection—like a vaccine? Once again, the answer lies in assessing your belief system. The process of examining our beliefs, adopting some and rejecting others, does not follow a simple, straight-line course. You may consciously revise your beliefs about what matters in your life, choosing, for example, to value creative opportunities over greater security. (My husband, a freelance writer, did this when he left a regular job to strike out on his own.) However, one choice doesn't end the debate inside your heart and mind. You may forever be affected by old *shoulds*, and their remnants could have more to do with how you feel than anything said by another person.

Conflicts between old and new beliefs will arise throughout your life. They are especially common in intimate relationships. When someone who really matters to you inadvertently touches an old emotional sore spot, the pain can be terrible. (A common example:

When you were a child your parents commented on everything you ate. Now when your husband asks if you want more food, you feel anger, guilt, and shame.)

Recovering from old, toxic beliefs depends on what you truly believe about yourself now and what matters in your life. There will always be people who will offer their opinions, usually based on standards authorized by the U.S. of G. The best antidote is a fully developed set of your own values and beliefs that are not generic, but tailor-made by you. Then you'll be on the path of feeling Real.

A Final Word About Feelings

Feelings are so devalued in our society that emotional confusion is truly epidemic. As children, we experience our feelings in a clear and unfettered way. When we grow up they become so mixed-up—I like to say "adulterated"—that we can have trouble just attaching a word to what's in our hearts at any moment.

When you get stuck and just don't know what you

feel, this list may help. Find a quiet place, sit with the list, and consider which of the feelings seem to be at play within you. It's an especially effective tool for all you Betty Blands who have been trained to go numb in a variety of situations.

The Feelings List

abandoned	confused	exuberant	inconsolable
abused	creative	failing	independent
aggravated	dependent	fragile	insecure
angry	depressed	frustrated	irritable
anxious	determined	grandiose	itchy
aroused	dirty	grateful	jealous
ashamed	disconnected	happy	jumpy
attractive	distracted	helpful	lazy
blank	distraught	helpless	lethargic
bored	dizzy	hopeful	lost
childlike	drained	hopeless	loving
clean	elated	horrified	manic
cold	empty	impatient	miserable
comfortable	excited	incompetent	nauseous

nervous	powerless	stingy	vulnerable
numb	quiet	suspicious	wise
open	restless	thrilled	wistful
overwhelmed	sad	tired	withdrawn
pained	sedated	uncomfortable	
perplexed	sexy	violent	

Keep this list handy for those moments of confusion, and feel free to add any that I may have left out. Every language on Earth includes dozens and dozens of words that represent human emotions. This alone should tell us that no part of life is more important.

Velveteen

Principle #4

Real Women Are Empathetic

On a recent visit with my grown daughter in Chicago, I made sure to go with her to the famous Shedd Aquarium, where one of our favorite creatures in the world—a green sea turtle named Nickel—bobs around the Caribbean Reef exhibit with parrot fish, angelfish, and puffers. Nickel swims a bit strangely—her rear end bounces upward as if it's being pulled by a balloon. When we saw her, some nearby children were reacting to Nickel's odd behavior with a mixture of judgment and confusion.

"Look at that weird turtle."

"The way it swims is retarded."

"What's wrong with it?"

Then one of the girls in the group spotted a sign that told the turtle's story. As she read it aloud, the children learned that Nickel had been found adrift off the Gulf Coast of Florida. Almost dead because of a big gash in her shell from a boat propeller, she was rescued by marine biologists and nursed back to health. During an exam, the biologists discovered that the turtle had swallowed a nickel (hence her name) and that the coin had likely caused the nerve damage responsible for her strange way of swimming. The injury is permanent, and Nickel never would have survived if she were returned to the sea. But at the aquarium she thrives, seemingly unaware of her disability.

Once they heard Nickel's story, the children spoke about her in a completely different way. One said it was "way cool" that she had survived the propeller strike, and another admired the effort she put into swimming despite her disability. They all agreed that she was beautiful, courageous, and strong.

What force transformed their attitudes? In a word—empathy. Once the children had come to know Nickel a little better, through her story, they couldn't judge her harshly. Understanding her experience had made the children see her not as a generic turtle, but as an individual with feelings and a history that they could connect with in an intimate way. Their change of heart at the Caribbean Reef exhibit was a perfect illustration of how empathy helps all of us to be Real.

Empathy allows us to feel deep appreciation and respect. When we have empathy, we are curious about the experiences, feelings, and values that shape a person's life. Empathy moves us beyond gender, status, and appearance to discover the Real and valuable person. It gives us a level of understanding that makes us feel connected and safe.

Unfortunately, empathy is not often valued or cultivated in the Object Culture, where everyone is supposed to be generically perfect. Few of us are taught to approach others with a positive empathetic point of view. Fewer still learn that to be Real, we must begin by having empathy for ourselves. Instead, families teach girls that they must grow up to be selfless caretakers for partners, children, aged parents, and even siblings. Communicated through *shoulds*, these lessons can make us feel as if we're responsible for everyone and everything around us.

A similar dynamic predominates in the world of work. Historically, which fields have traditionally offered the most opportunity for women? Teaching, nursing, social work, and childcare held places on a very short list. All require the one big skill universally ascribed to women—caretaking. If women were to be found outside these occupations in, say, business, they almost always played supporting roles as secretaries or administrative assistants. Again, they were supposed to take care of others—not take care of themselves.

Fortunately, today's women may have more opportunities in life—and more chances to *choose* empathy—rather than having no choices other than caretaking jobs. Careers once denied us are now available. But even though things are better in many ways, the power of Other People's Opinions still demands that we neglect ourselves and care for others to the point of exhaustion. We work hard in the outside world even as we still do most of the caretaking at home. All this effort can be draining and contributes to anxiety, depression, and burnout.

I call victims of this cycle "Women Who Care Too Much." The syndrome is widespread and growing. And it is the product of too much concern for OPO and our own powerful desires to do good. In the rush to be caretakers and escape the judgments of the Object Culture and other people, we fail to learn the emotional skill—empathy—that is an essential precursor to accepting and embracing our Real selves and others.

Care vs. Empathy

When you care about someone or something, you make an emotional investment. It matters to you if a friend or family member feels well and is happy. You can have similar feelings about a pet or even a baseball team. Tune in to a sports talk show, and you'll very quickly learn how much some people care about the local team.

Caring may also involve providing a service for others. As women, we perform countless acts of caring every day, from feeding the dog to transporting an aspiring ballerina to her dance school. Running errands, cooking meals, shopping, and soothing bruised shins and egos are all caring actions. We care for ourselves, as well as others, with the right food, rest, and exercise. Self-care, whether it takes the form of daily applications of sunscreen or a weekly pottery class, is essential to our health and happiness.

But caring is not the same as empathy. Caring is a little more removed. It can be practiced in a generic way, and it doesn't require that you truly know another person's background, emotions, values, and experiences.

Every child on Earth needs care in the form of food and shelter, for example.

However, if you want to get past the superficial and connect with people as individuals, you have to learn about their special, idiosyncratic needs, interests, and desires. This is the difference between caring and empathy. Empathy is specific and idiosyncratic, and it depends on being receptive to all that makes a person an individual.

With the exception of those who have been so hurt in the past that they prefer to hide away, most human beings yearn to be seen and understood clearly. We want to know we are recognized as one-of-a-kind individuals, and we hope others have enough empathy to care for us in a unique and not generic way. (For example, if I'm going to take care of myself, I need more than a toothbrush. I need things like art supplies for my creative side and a cozy bedroom, complete with a friendly cat, for rest.)

In Margery Williams's story of the Velveteen Rabbit, the little Boy demonstrated remarkable empathy for the stuffed bunny, who is the central character in the book. He made sure that Rabbit, who longed to be Real, could explore tunnels made in the bedclothes that were just like a real rabbit warren. The Boy also took the bunny outside, where he could play like a flesh-and-blood rabbit. Once, when the Boy's Nana referred to the bunny as a "toy," he responded, "You mustn't say that. He isn't a toy. He's Real!"

If the Boy had simply cared for Rabbit in a generic way, he might have made sure it was kept clean and was put away properly after he played with it. But because he recognized what was in the bunny's heart, the Boy felt true empathy. His caring involved helping the bunny to feel closer to his individual dream of becoming Real. His empathy was so strong that when Nana didn't see how special this rabbit was, he had to shout.

The Empathy Deficit

The Boy's empathy for the Velveteen Rabbit and the empathy eventually shown by the children at the Shedd Aquarium for beautiful Nickel, the turtle, move us because they illustrate something rare. In the U.S. of G., genuine empathy based on a deep appreciation for people as unique individuals has such a low value that we don't even think about it. Worst of all, it's missing where we need it the most: in our families.

This is true even though human survival depends on a parent's instinctive, empathetic response to a baby's cry. This instinct is responsible for the overwhelming sense of protectiveness and concern most mothers and fathers feel from the moment their children are born. But soon enough, as parents are bombarded with advice on how to mold their children and warnings about spoiling them, many start losing their appreciation for their children's unique characters. Some parents fear that their daughter's fate depends, in part, on her ability to comply with social standards. Soon enough they start to ignore her signals and push her to conform to the little girl ideal.

It's hard to imagine a relationship problem that has caused more damage to more people than the erosion of parent–child empathy. All of our basic beliefs about ourselves and others are established early in life. A parent's empathy and attention confirm our value. When they're missing, or worse, replaced by judgment, neglect, or abuse, the damage is deep and long lasting. If, time after time, your feelings and desires are ignored or discounted, you come to believe that you are powerless, and the world is cold and uncaring.

These parents are not trying to hurt their children. They are themselves insecure. They hope that by treating their daughters like generic little girls, they might somehow get it right. When I was a young mother, I saw this happen with toilet training. The other mothers I knew seemed to compete over whose child got out of diapers first. With so much pressure on them, their children suffered far more stress, not to mention accidents, which were interpreted as their children's earliest failures.

The problem is that not every child is capable of meeting generic milestones and standards of behavior. And if they do, perchance, meet such a standard, so what? Generic achievements have nothing to do with a child's unique abilities and qualities. If a mother is truly empathetic, shouldn't she encourage her daughter to meet her own individual milestones? I know one empathetic mom who celebrates each of her son's steps toward speech, and because he was born with a cleft palate, his progress is unique. Instead of starting out with strong syllables like Da-Da-Da, he creates sounds in the back of his throat. But these noises are just as important and just as worthy of approval as any baby's pre-speech sounds.

Unfortunately, many parents do not empathize with or recognize their children's particular developmental achievements, but instead pressure their kids to conform to generic standards. A girl raised this way ends up judging herself against an unrealistic ideal. She feels like she is a "good" girl when she comes close to complying and a "bad" girl when she fails. Of course we carry this pattern into adulthood and constantly measure ourselves against the Object Culture's standards. Because the standards are unreasonable, we rarely satisfy them and almost always feel inadequate when we don't measure up to the sameness expected of us.

If we're all the same, then all we need is basic caretaking. This empathy-free, nonspecific way of relating to others is practically epidemic. It's especially easy to see in some marriages. Take the husband who loves his wife and shows his feelings by fixing the leaky showerhead in the bathroom. He expects her deep appreciation because he believes all women ache for all men to repair things. She's grateful, but then complains that his obsession with his work makes him seem cold and withdrawn. If he had true empathy for her, he would understand that she needs an emotional connection more than she needs good water pressure. She could get that from a plumber.

As I mentioned, the empathy deficit reaches its most extreme when we can no longer feel empathy for ourselves. Many women suffer from this problem. They are the ones who hardly ever express an opinion, a request, or a need. When they do, they apologize first—"I'm sorry to ask this, but . . ."—and then expect to be turned down.

I encountered a most heartrending example of the loss of self-empathy while I was working on this chapter. I met a dear friend, Nancy, for lunch. Five days before, she had suffered a miscarriage. But as she talked, she focused much more on how she had let others down than on her own feelings. When I said I wanted to treat her to a nourishing meal with dessert, Nancy resisted, saying she didn't deserve special treatment, couldn't afford the calories, and, besides, "I should be getting over it by now."

Shocked, I asked her, "How long would *you* give *me* to get over a miscarriage?"

"Oh, a couple of years, at least," Nancy said.

Her answer was correct. Any women would need a

long time to recover from a lost pregnancy, and most women would willingly allow a good friend to take as long as she needed to accommodate herself to such an upsetting event. Sadly, though, Nancy couldn't apply this reasonable, empathetic standard to herself. She was too caught up in all the *shoulds* she had been taught about caring for others.

Practicing Self-Empathy First

My friend Nancy was not so detached from her own experience that she couldn't see the point I made about self-empathy. She allowed me to take care of her by listening and feeding her, and she felt enough concern for her own situation that she was open to the idea of taking time to recover from what she had been through.

Nancy could recognize her own needs and move to meet them. In my psychotherapy practice, I've seen women who are so lacking in self-empathy that they don't seem to recognize they have needs of their own. And once you stop listening to your own heart—stop having empathy for yourself—it becomes difficult to hear the hearts of others and respond to them. Women who suffer this fate may still behave like caretakers. They cook, clean, and carpool, but they lack true empathy for others. They don't intend to act this way, and when they realize it's happening, they might even try harder in their generic caretaking duties. Instead, they need to take a break from all their scrambling and listen to the voice of their Real selves, which they have ignored for too long.

> OPO: *Oh, no, here we go. This is going to be one of those selfish, me, me, me messages. Most of what's wrong in the world today is caused by people who only care about themselves.*
>
> Toni: *Try to resist jumping to conclusions for once, OPO. Self-empathy is very different from selfishness. In fact, self-empathy gives you the skill and energy to be far more generous with others.*

Self-empathy begins with simply accepting that you deserve care and respect on an individualized basis. Your talents, interests, passions, dreams, and loves matter, and so do your own experiences in life. Just like

Nickel, the turtle, you have lived a unique story. Your wounds deserve care, and your aspirations deserve encouragement.

When you have respect for yourself, and when you recognize that by simply being born you merit individualized care, you can begin to nurture yourself in an empathic way. Some people call this caring for the "inner child." This is a helpful metaphor. It suggests that as we move through our days, we can speak to ourselves and treat ourselves with the kindness and gentleness we would afford a precious child.

OPO: *Oh, brother, now she wants us to be self-indulgent and childish.*

Toni: *Oh, brother, yourself. I'm not saying you have permission to be bratty or babyish. Just step outside yourself and be as understanding and patient with yourself as you might be with a kid you care about.*

As you start to care for your inner child, you have an opportunity to improve on the past. Chances are good that when you were young you received a lot of one-size-fits-all parenting and were expected to be grateful for it. What if, this time, you care for that little girl in a way that is tailored to her individual needs? You could tell her that she can live by her own Real beliefs and values, and reject the culture's imperatives. You could say, "So what if you're not perfect? I like you the way you are." You would listen as she tells you about her Real hopes and dreams, and conspire with her to make some of them come true.

Self-empathy requires you to accept that you are unique and acknowledge that you do not have to participate in the struggle to be generically perfect. It also involves recognizing how you may have been damaged by your upbringing and the negative messages of the Object Culture.

Often these traumas become a collection of small burdens—I call them your "Bag of Rocks." We all carry one. That Bag of Rocks can keep you from being happy about yourself and being Real if you buy into OPO and the standards of the U.S. of G.

What is in your Bag of Rocks? Most likely it contains several different fears—that you are ugly or stupid or damaged or unworthy. Your bag may also hold memories of feeling ashamed sometime in the past. It may also hold your anxieties about your personality, talents, or abilities. Got a terrible sense of direction? (I do!) How about a learning disability? (I do!) Come from a dysfunctional family? (Who doesn't?)

As you may have noticed, the "rocks" many of us carry are often labeled with qualities or traits that the U.S. of G. would find to be not "normal." In the generic way of looking at things, "normal" is bland, middle-of-the-road, superficially competent, and unblemished. It is also nonexistent. No one fits this definition. We all have strengths and weakness, gifts and imperfections. In fact, in a Real world, "normal" would be redefined to mean "imperfect" but genuinely human. Normal would include the Bag of Rocks that comes with every human life.

What's in Your Bag?

Experiences, feelings, thoughts, and attitudes that make us feel like we are not "normal" don't simply disappear from our hearts. Instead, we tend to collect them in our Bags of Rocks. And the weight of carrying them around makes it hard for us to grow and reach our goals in life. However, many of us have trouble identifying the rocks we carry. Fortunately, there's an exercise that helps.

Save a paper or plastic bag from the grocery store. Hunt down a marking pen, some scraps of paper, and some rubber bands. Then go to the park, the beach, or your backyard and collect some stones. (If there are none handy, don't worry, the paper can be a substitute.)

Once you have a quiet place where you won't be disturbed, make a pile of your rocks and pick up the pen. Then, one by one, on each of the rocks write a word or two that represents a supposed flaw or abnormality that bothers you. If you need more than a few words, write a description on a piece of paper and wrap it around the stone with a rubber band.

Take your time. Stop if necessary and go back to it later. And don't worry about finishing. You may think of new words to put on your rocks at any time. If you do, just go ahead and do it.

Eventually, you will have a fairly heavy little bag (or one filled with lots of pieces of paper).

When you are finished, give yourself a moment to feel the weight of the bag and notice the number of rock you possess. After you have done this, consider, if you can, the true nature of rocks.

Rocks are solid, strong, stable, and enduring. Rocks are used to build foundations for houses and statues to honor great people. Rocks pave our roads, and some, when they are cut and polished, become jewels. Rocks are not shameful. They are not normal or abnormal. They are simply part of the earth, and without them, life as we know it would be impossible.

The same is true for your Bag of Rocks. Yes, they may represent struggle and pain. But they also stand for experiences that, interpreted with empathy, have made you unique. Your rocks are not just a burden. They also stand for the foundation of your Real self, and they can be used for building self-empathy and a new definition of "normal" that includes every stone in the bag.

A warning about the "rocks" exercise: It is most important to practice self-empathy when you reflect on your past, especially the painful aspects of your personal history. A great many women feel shame about things they did or didn't do in times gone by. Some women I know condemn themselves for having had too many sexual partners, for example. Others decide they were prudes because they had so few. But isn't it possible that the choices you made were the best you could make at the time? Couldn't you make an effort to understand the woman you once were and accept her without criticism? Won't you accept that people, all people, are imperfect, and that life is sometimes a messy, confusing, and contradictory process? And besides, what if you were or even are promiscuous or a prude? What punishment does that Thinglish label merit?

OPO: *Slut! Ice queen!*
Toni: *Enough name-calling—that doesn't do anyone any good!*
OPO: *It makes me feel superior to put people in categories.*

When women consider the idea of self-empathy, they sometimes confuse it with selfishness. Self-empathy has nothing to do with greed or self-centeredness. Instead, self-empathy calls you to treat yourself with compassion and to respect your personal history, your temperament, your talents, and your shortcomings. After all, how can you be truly empathic with others if you don't practice empathy with yourself? And why should anyone else have empathy for you if you don't practice positive self-regard?

Empathy for Others

Once you truly embrace your Real self, including your Bag of Rocks, a remarkable thing starts to happen: You develop the ability to see and appreciate others as they Really are. You see their Bags of Rocks (the way the kids at the Shedd Aquarium saw Nickel's past struggles), and you find you want to nurture them as unique individuals.

Women who have empathy for themselves don't suffer from the burnout that comes with trying to satisfy

OPO. For example, a mother who accepts her own teenage past with empathy (including the mistakes she made) is less likely to demand that her own adolescent daughter be a perfect generic kid. Instead, she'll be able to see her Real daughter, and she'll take care of her with so much empathy that she can love her through anything.

With a partner or husband, self-empathy can make us far more receptive to the idiosyncratic needs of the one we've chosen to walk with us through life. With empathy, we can get specific. For example, while most men may feel pampered and loved when presented with a beef brisket, an empathic woman will know whether such an entrée works with her particular man. Similarly, a dozen roses might charm many women, but there are some who hate roses. When you have empathy for others, you do not assume you know how they feel. Instead, you slow down, ask questions, and listen carefully to the answers. Once you truly understand what another person feels and desires, you have options. You can practice empathy.

Returning to the parent–child relationship, which can be a most empathetic bond, we can see the process at work when some very basic issues arise. Consider the matter of getting kids to eat vegetables. The social norm says that we must present our children with every vegetable you can buy in the market and require them to eat each one. But science tells us that a child's taste buds are extremely sensitive and can be overwhelmed by flavors that adults enjoy. We also know that battling with young children over food can contribute to serious issues (like eating disorders) later on.

What is the empathetic solution? Should you stand over your child, demanding she gag down her spinach? Should a child remain seated and isolated at the table until she finishes? Though parents use both these approaches, neither shows much empathy for a child's feelings or health. A more empathetic strategy might involve keeping track of the vegetables your child does like and serving them as often as possible. You can also experiment with recipes to see if you can broaden the list or offer alternatives—celery sticks on a day when you eat Brussels sprouts—and a multivitamin. Be creative, not punitive. Maybe your daughter will eat what she helps cook, or maybe she's happier to eat something playfully called "baby trees," while she rejects a thing called broccoli.

Yes, the more empathetic approach requires a little

extra effort and flexibility, which is a hallmark of empathy. But the payoff can be great. First, day-to-day events at the table become less stressful. Second, your connection with your child becomes stronger because you know her better. Third, you may well escape food issues in the future because you didn't turn veggies into a power struggle.

In the workplace, empathy continues to work wonders. An art teacher I know has seen the effects of empathy in her classroom so many times that it has become her favorite tool for helping students who get stuck on a lesson. She learned this when she worked with a special-needs student who struggled with the concept of perspective (creating a sense of space and distance) in pictures. While others were able to use different-sized shapes to make things seem closer or farther away, this boy had trouble getting past the fact that to him the shapes all looked like turtles. When his teacher gave him permission to draw a pond on his paper and arrange the turtles to show things in natural-looking perspective, he mastered the lesson. His success came about when she listened and adjusted her teaching methods to his needs. That is empathy in action. It left both teacher and student feeling good, and it established a working relationship that could lead to future successes.

The empathy process—asking questions, listening for answers, crafting creative responses—works in all sorts of relationships. If you work with others at a job, a little bit of empathy will help with team projects and all your relationships on the job. Empathy helps reduce conflicts and makes most people happier about going to work. It's always better to spend time with people who are more than objects, more than fellow employees.

In every context, when you show empathy for others, it helps them feel safe, understood, and at ease. People who feel this way are more likely to be happy and to grow. Empathy even sees us through those little moments in life when a mishap or misunderstanding could cause trouble.

Think about the last time a clerk in a store treated you rudely, or a server dumped coffee or soup in your lap. What if, in the moment of possible conflict, you imagined the Bag of Rocks that person carried each day? What if you had empathy for her struggle to make a living or care for others? Empathy would lead you to conclude "She's doing the best she can." If you can pull it off, this empathetic response would save both of you from hard feelings. You might even squeeze a laugh out of the situation.

Becoming an Empathy Role Model

s Real women move through life, they can affect others in many positive ways. When we show empathy directly, we affirm other people's worth and give them the kind of care—specific, not generic—that helps them in a meaningful way. We also help others if we demonstrate that we have empathy for ourselves.

Being a role model for self-empathy is especially important if you are someone's mother. You are your child's example. She's watching you all the time and learning how to think about herself and her place in the world. She hears when you say "I should just kill myself" in response to day-to-day challenges. How do you think these comments affect her? If you want your child to grow into a woman who recognizes her worth as a person and empathizes with others, then you will demonstrate self-empathy and not self-criticism in an open and matter-of-fact way.

The practice of self-empathy has been extremely important in my relationship with my daughters. When they were young and very impressionable, they complained that I wasn't like some of the mothers they met at friends' homes or the ones on TV, who were stunningly beautiful, shopped, baked, and exercised a lot more than I did. Their complaints hurt sometimes. Being Real is a never-ending process, and I was susceptible to the culture's messages about the "perfect mother," who was endlessly cheery and conventionally beautiful as she skipped from a soccer game to a dinner party without smearing her mascara. Sometimes I tried to comply with the standard, running myself ragged and feeling like a failure because I just couldn't do everything. But the stress of this effort—something most women have felt—was so great that I realized my Real self was suffering. I had to recognize that the perfect mother was a myth, and my version of good enough was good enough. With my own physical and mental health at stake, I tried to respond to my daughters with empathy, but I also demonstrated self-empathy by limiting my efforts. I wanted them to learn that life held endless possibilities, not just the object standards of the Perfect Object Woman.

In time, my daughters grew to see beyond the superficial qualities they saw in other women and media messages. They also learned to see the value in my mothering style. I didn't serve a lot of cake and cookies, but I did everything I could to help them be Real. I taught them that they were worthy, and I helped them develop into unique individuals who recognized the toxic, limiting messages of the Object Culture and valued themselves.

My daughters' development affirmed my belief in what is Real. It also opened my eyes to the positive cycle that flows when we practice empathy for ourselves and others. As young adults, my daughters have shown themselves to be remarkably empathetic with friends, family members, children in their care, and even me. Empathy has helped them to be Real.

Nowadays, after the storms of their adolescence have passed, my daughters and I joke about their years of tormenting me to become a sporty size-2 shopping mom preparing Rice Krispies Treats while wearing sparkly scarves and sipping mint tea. It was a long process, but what a relief to be seen gently and clearly for my Real self.

The cycle of empathy—breeding empathy—works in wonderful ways for my daughters, too. They try to be sensitive to what is Real in others and respond to them in specific, not generic, ways. And when they fall offtrack in their own lives, as we all do, they understand that they must listen to their own hearts, respect their own values and desires, and live as individuals—rocks and all.

Velveteen

Principle #5

Real Women Are Courageous

I t's great that there are women who hurtle into space aboard rockets, throw themselves down mountains on skis, and otherwise risk their lives by moving forward, even when they are afraid. However, you don't have to overcome a big physical challenge or endure a grueling test of stamina to demonstrate the kind of courage that Real women practice every day. Sometimes all you have to do is tell the truth to your mother or your daughter or yourself.

Personal courage is essential to being Real. It is also a quality or character trait that seems to grow stronger the more we use it. Over the years, I have found that one of the best ways to explore how Real women relate to each other with courage involves a frank discussion of the most important, perilous, and rewarding relationship—the one between a mother and a daughter.

Nearly all of us have had mothers of some sort in our lives, and thus have had a place on at least one side of this equation. (A great many of us actually sit in the middle, between our mothers and our daughters.) And most women would agree that the relationship between mother and daughter is one of the most intense, challenging, and potentially rewarding connections two human beings can experience. Certainly, great writers and filmmakers believe this is true because they produce countless works that examine the mother–daughter dynamic.

What makes it so profound? First, it begins even before a daughter is born, as a mother invests enormous emotional energy into the child who grows inside her. Once she is born, an infant's attachment to her mother is immediate and complete. Likewise, a mother also feels a heady mixture of love, protectiveness, and hope. She cannot help but imagine a future for this girl, and even if she is determined to avoid the pitfalls that come with pride and ambition, she will feel that her daughter's life will be a reflection of her own.

Other factors contribute to the power of the mother-daughter bond. As most people acknowledge and neuroscience has recently confirmed, girls and women are naturally inclined toward empathy and can be expected to focus on relationships. Repeated studies of gender differences have found women to be more sensitive to social interactions, better able to determine another person's emotions, and more skilled at expressing their own feelings than men. These are average differences, and exceptions are common. But in general, they support a common belief that the mother–daughter relationship tends to be more intense, emotionally charged, and complex than many other types of relationships.

In the beginning, little girls and their moms generally enjoy plenty of mutual interests and affection. But over time, as incidents, comments, expectations, and disappointments add up, a great many mother–daughter pairs feel the strain. As daughters grow into women and young mothers mature, they often grow apart. However, if they are Real, mothers and daughters can negotiate these changes and allow their relationship to change in a positive way. It takes courage to make this happen. And the kind of bravery exhibited by the gutsiest mothers and daughters shows how we can all have courageously Real relationships with others.

Seeing Yourself Clearly

Therapists and counselors work with a great many teenage daughters and their mothers. Because the challenge of adolescence is so well-known, many adults look to developmental issues for the source of trouble in the relationship. Everyone knows that teens are sometimes erratic, confused, inconsistent, and emotional because they are going through so many physical, social, and developmental changes. Of course, the parent is more likely to say, "She's a brat. We can't even have a conversation any more. She hates me."

What people say about teens is true. But adolescence isn't the only time when we must deal with profound change. Mothers of adolescent girls are going through changes, too. They must adapt to their own aging and physical maturity in addition to the effects these factors have on their emotions. And both mothers and daughters face the vexing matter of learning to deal with what is Real as they change and grow.

The first step in working out any problem in a relationship is a courageous look at yourself. This is the case not just for parents and children, but in all relationships where you might have longstanding conflicts or feel tension when you deal with someone. In my work with mothers and daughters, I've found that a simple phrase—"embarrassing moments"—can jumpstart one's self-evaluation.

Ask a mother when she has felt most embarrassed by

her daughter, and she's likely to recall her child's shocking attempt at a new hair color, a moment when her daughter said something outlandish in front of other people or, perhaps, a failure at school that brought mother and daughter together in the principal's office. They repeat phrases like "Why didn't I know this?" (a perfect mother is supposed to know everything) and "Why didn't she come to me?"

Daughters answer the most-embarrassing-moment question in remarkably similar ways. They almost always say that they felt embarrassed because of something their moms did or said or how they looked in front of classmates or friends. Desperate to differentiate themselves from their mothers, many daughters will become aggressive critics, muttering judgments such as "I can't stand to be seen with her" and "I can't believe how she dresses."

Think for a moment about the similarities in what mothers and daughters have to say about each other. In almost every case, the complaints have an Object orientation. This is because embarrassment always involves our fear of OPO. It requires that we care about what other people think of us and our children. And it often arises when we fear that someone isn't measuring up to a certain social standard. This, too, is a sign that we are not taking a Real view, not seeing with empathy. Perhaps we are even expecting our daughters (or moms) to grant us a measure of Object status by coming closer to the culture's ideal.

It's a courageous act to admit this difficult truth and begin to work on it. (I describe the process as "feel it, face it, fix it.") And you'll find little support for dealing with relationship issues in the United States of Generica. The Object Culture actually teaches us to be cowardly when it comes to dealing with emotional and personal issues. This is why so many women practice heart-numbing activities—overindulging in drugs, alcohol, sex, shopping, etc. They act AS If (Absent, Superficial, Insecure, and Fearful) because no one has shown them how to bravely face their difficulties, and they are afraid that the process will be painful.

Well, I cannot lie. The truth, especially when it's about ourselves, can hurt. It's painful, for example, to admit you have trouble accepting your daughter for who she Really is. I know one mother, Anna, who had to face the fact that she continually criticized her daughter Diane's eating habits because she secretly wanted her child to be a skinny, admired POW. Anna also had certain competitive feelings—wanting her daughter to be a more successful Object than others. The result, as you might expect, was tension in their relationship, constant conflict over food, and a steady deterioration in the relationship.

As she looked even more closely at herself, Anna took the risk to recognize that as a girl she had been measured against unfair Object standards and was made to feel inadequate by her own mother. Painful memories of incidents and parental messages that shape our self-image are hard to avoid when we bravely consider why we carry certain attitudes and expectations through life. But understanding the source is central to addressing any problem.

The key to fixing things with her daughter was Anna's brave effort to consider that she had applied Object standards to Diane and lost sight of her child's Real value. Of course, this mom had feelings of guilt about her attitudes. But by accessing self-empathy, she was able to recognize that she had been influenced by powerful cultural norms (we all fall under that spell sometimes, don't we?) and didn't have to beat herself up over it. She could move from feelings of regret and self-criticism to adopt a new, more positive and accepting view of her daughter, who just happened to be a brilliant, compassionate, and delightfully funny young woman.

As so often happens, one person's courage inspires another to take the same path. Once she felt that her mother was being Real and showing empathy, Diane began to consider that she had some pretty unRealistic ideas about her mom. She had been holding her mother up to impossible standards, expecting her to be perfectly understanding, attuned, and flawless in the way she communicated. Slowly, Diane worked up the courage to let go of these high standards and appreciate her Real mother. Both women were rewarded with a much closer and more positive relationship.

I know from personal experience that this process works. My two daughters, Elizabeth and Amy, have taught me that I need to focus on what really matters— core values, character, communication—and to stop worrying about superficial things like their piercings and tattoos. I have taught them that they should never expect perfection from anyone (mom included), but that within each imperfect person is much to cherish and enjoy. And since courage is inherently optimistic, it helps us all to expect positive interactions and positive outcomes whenever we take risks.

A word of warning: Don't assume that everything can be fixed. Yes, I have seen mothers and daughters in extreme circumstances—where violence, drug abuse, and serious mental illness cloud the picture—find ways to connect. But sadly, sometimes these relationships cannot be repaired because the cause of the pain remains. When this happens, a woman may have to be courageous enough to stop trying to accomplish the impossible and move on.

The Courage to Say No

At many points in our lives, courageous self-examination can move us toward saying "yes" to ourselves, to another person, to a relationship. Just as rewarding and important is the courage to say "no" when necessary.

For many women, the courage to say no can be very difficult to summon up because it violates one of the Object Culture's primary messages to women: You must always please others. The ways women must please are too numerous to count, but here are just a few:

Be pleasing to look at.
Be pleasing to deal with.
Say "please" even when it's not necessary.
Give others sensual pleasure through cooking, home-
making, even sex.

These examples, and more, are among the many
shoulds that run women's lives. Many of us internalize
these messages and hound ourselves with the same
impossible demands. Whenever we hear the word
should, it is an alarm telling us that our freedom of
choice is at stake. I recommend replacing it with the
word *could*, which immediately provides you with
options. And for that inner voice that issues an endless
stream of *shoulds*, I would prescribe one of the few
strict commandments for Real women: *Thou shalt not
should thyself.*

Even if we realize that it's possible to say no to a
should, we often can't bring ourselves to do it. We are
afraid of offending or hurting. And we are afraid of
being rejected and labeled something horrible—selfish
bitch, maybe?—that will cause others to reject us. For
this reason, many women tiptoe around conflicts and
constantly seek permission from others—saying

"please"—when it's completely unnecessary.

Women develop a host of problems when they constantly try to please others. For one thing, they lose the integrity to assert themselves in a productive way. (As Margaret Thatcher explained, "If you just set out to be liked, you would be prepared to compromise on anything at any time, and you would achieve nothing.") Women who always please, even when it's not their choice to do so, also tend to develop unspoken resentments. This feeling invariably shows itself. We become a little impatient, a little edgy, a little angry, and then guilty for being angry, and around and around it goes.

But what if you were brave enough just to consider whether you should do all the pleasing things others expect? What if you had the courage to risk short-term disapproval by using the word *no*? At first, you might meet resistance or even anger. But done gently and with empathy and openness, we can say no and still have good relationships. For example, you can say, "No, I can't make a special meal for you tonight, and you can use the kitchen to cook what you like," or "I'm not available to help you with that problem right now, but let's arrange a time to work on it."

The key is having as much respect and empathy for

yourself as you have for others. You can then bravely and without hostility state your choice and leave an opening for others to solve their own problems or reconnect with you later. This kind of "no" is good for you and good for others, too. A child who makes her own sandwich learns self-sufficiency. The same is true for a husband who has to communicate with his son, without your intervening or playing interpreter.

I know it can be difficult to take a stand this way. For this reason I recommend a practice I call "bathtub therapy." It allows you to take a courageous stand, then step away from a situation so that others can solve their own problems.

Bathtub Therapy

Courage is fortified when asserting control over our own lives. Sometimes there's no better— and maybe no other—way to do this other than a long hot soak in the privacy of the bathtub.

Because it is secluded, private, and relatively free of distractions, the bathtub can be a wonderful place to reconnect with yourself. Bathtub therapy, as I call it, allows us to rest, meditate, and reconnect with our true selves while letting go of *shoulds* and tuning out OPO. It's also easy.

Fill the tub with water warmed to a relaxing temperature, then let the faucet run just enough to maintain the heat and create a relaxing sound.

Undress and slip into the water. In this tub you do not have to satisfy anyone's demands, deadlines, or requirements.

With your eyes closed, allow yourself to relax each muscle in your body.

Let your breathing settle into an even, easy rhythm.

Once you feel calm and at peace, let your mind imagine your best life, a life in which your Real self is expressed and your Real needs are met.

Every woman finds a different set of hopes and dreams during bathtub therapy, and the specific elements may change over time. But one thing is consistent in this exercise: The Real you and the Best Life that emerges from the warm water meditation deserve your attention. Granting yourself this gift will also give you the peace, energy, and motivation to have empathy for others.

I practiced a lot of bathtub therapy when my children were young, and I was overstressed and often confused. At that time, the bathroom was the most reliable refuge in the house, and the sound of the running water drowned out the sounds of my daughters and their father, so I could get a moment of peace.

During these moments of therapy, I sometimes tried to think about my professional future, but my mind would go blank. I would worry that I lacked direction. So I began, very slowly, to imagine my best future. I asked myself, "What would I want to wear to work?" I wondered, "What kind of place would I like to work in?" And "What kind of services would be provided, and how would I be treated?"

Each bath got me closer to knowing what specifically suited me as a Real person. Each one also contributed to the development of the life I have today.

Redefine Please

Often the final milestone for women who adopt a more courageous approach to life involves letting go of the impulse to constantly say "please." This word is a type of social grease that keeps things running smoothly, and good manners require us to say it in many situations. But do you find yourself saying please as part of seeking permission to do things that normal adults are free to choose for themselves? For example, no woman needs to ask permission to see friends she loves. Nor does she need permission to pursue outlets for her creative, emotional, or spiritual needs.

If you continually ask for things that are reasonably yours or seek permission from others in order to be yourself, try to imagine why. Are you afraid? Do you want others to make key decisions for you? (This is a way of escaping responsibility for your life.) Or is it just a stubborn habit? If so, I suggest you adopt a new definition for PLEASE based on this acronym:

Permission to
Live
Every day
As a
Self-designed
Experience

The Courage to Be Yourself

Strange as it may sound, courage is a by-product of fear. Think about it—does it take courage to do something that doesn't scare you? Of course not. So being afraid doesn't mean you lack courage. Once you acknowledge the fear (which in itself is a gutsy maneuver), then you have a choice as to how you wish to respond. Each time you choose courage and prevail over fear, you make yourself a little bit stronger and a little bit braver. This is precisely the path the Velveteen Rabbit followed in Margery Williams's book. He asked, "Does it hurt?" when the Skin Horse talked about becoming Real, and the answer was "Sometimes." But he moved ahead anyway, letting one courageous step lead him to another.

A very moving story about this kind of courage was posted on the Velveteen Principles website by a woman who goes by the screen name Little Dragonfly. She wrote:

On September 29, 2005, I took my life back . . . meaning, I finally admitted to myself after ten-plus years of denial that I was bulimic and had lost control of my life/body. I call that date above my "life day" because it was then that I saw what I was doing wasn't working, and I have since then begun a fierce moral inventory and found myself in the loving care of some beautiful, healthy people who have been more than encouraging through my recovery.

My eating disorder had grown into a vast hideous monster, and I buckled under it . . . marinating in self-hatred and pity . . . but I remember when my therapist and I sat down in one of our meetings that she asked me what I had missed out on in my life because of my eating disorder . . . I remember saying exactly, "I miss me" . . . I missed being the creative unique soul that I had covered up and tried to forget. . . .

As of today I am a "recovering bulimic" and

have been binge/purge-free for over a month and feeling more alive today . . . Your book has given me such a lovely, creative childhood story to view my own life . . . Being "Real" has allowed me not to experience shame of my own existence and individuality . . . The eating disorder fed and metastasized over my personal "shame" . . . but to embrace and treasure my uniqueness, now that is truly a novel concept . . . and I look forward to growing and appreciating this part of me for years to come. . . .

Yes, I am ragged and my ears have turned gray, but I feel more Real with each passing day . . . and so grateful for just the chance to live, change, and grow . . .

Once they develop the courage to consider their own behavior and to say yes and no when necessary, Real women can bravely be themselves with much less fear and hesitation. Notice I didn't say *no* fear or hesitation. But with courage, you can make your own values a priority and muster the strength to be Real. Here are just a few ways you can express courage.

The courage to stand alone. On many occasions you will not be one of the crowd, and that takes bravery. If someone pushes you to abandon your principles just to go along with the crowd, remember what the writer Alice Walker says: "No person is your friend who demands your silence, or denies your right to grow."

The courage to disappoint others. My daughter Elizabeth gave up music even when others expected her to go on to a career with a major orchestra. She had to bravely risk negative responses from others—OPO—in order to be free to live the life she chose.

The courage to tell the truth. Mothers and daughters will know and love each other better when they tell the truth. The same rule applies in every relationship because telling the truth lets people see the Real you.

The courage to change. The course of life—as we all age, grow, and face challenges—makes constant demands on us. Women who can stop judging themselves and others and adapt to what is Real will have richer lives and more meaningful relationships.

The courage to adopt new beliefs. Wouldn't it feel good to decide that you are worthy, lovable, and beautiful just as you are? These beliefs, and many more positive values, are available to you if you bravely embrace them.

The courage to be different. Decades ago, social scientists noted that women are trained to act, live, and even find careers within a very narrow range of options. They called it the *homogenization* of women. The pressure women face to conform is enormous. Breaking out requires great courage.

It's almost impossible to overstate the importance of courage in our lives and the danger we court when we withdraw and deny ourselves. Half of all women will suffer from cardiovascular disease in their lifetimes.

Some of this epidemic can be traced to stress and misery that can constrict our arteries (and our Realness) and contribute to a "heart attack." What an interesting metaphor! Our hearts are broken from a lack of Real joy and authenticity and peace with ourselves.

One of the preventive strategies we can employ against heartbreak is to live bravely. Courage allows us to put empathy into action on behalf of others and ourselves. It helps us to be Real in an assertive way. Courage doesn't always come naturally. At first you may have to talk yourself into being brave. But it is a transforming thing, for you and others who will follow your example. And like every useful muscle, it grows with exercise. "You gain strength, courage, and confidence by every experience in which you really stop to look fear in the face," said Eleanor Roosevelt. "You must do the thing which you think you cannot do."

Velveteen

Principle #6

Real Women Are Honest

My husband used to become annoying and incompetent—and frankly unbearable— on a monthly basis. Then I became more honest about having PMS. Suddenly, he stopped being a jerk for a short time every month. As a result, we had a much better chance to be happy together—he even became more empathetic about the challenges of hormones—every day of the month.

If you had a bit of courage and were once honest with someone about any of your personal imperfections, I bet you had a similar experience. Honesty leads to understanding. This is especially true when we admit our "imperfections" (as if perfect is possible). Deep down, most people have a basic desire to be empathetic, and when you take a risk and reveal your struggles—I playfully call this "showing your soft underbelly"—others will generally reward you with kindness. In *The Velveteen Rabbit*, for instance, the Skin Horse generously offered his wisdom and encouragement after the bunny was honest about his insecurities and his desire to be Real.

But in a culture that drives us to be perfect and generically agreeable, it is hard to speak the truth about ourselves and our feelings. Why? One reason is that we are desperate to *please* others. When you are gripped by this desire, you will hide the truth about your feelings whenever you disagree with someone. Eventually, this strategy for getting along becomes so ingrained that you automatically form opinions based on what others say instead of your own values.

We also hide the truth when we are terrified that we aren't living up to the standards of the U.S. of G. Consider my less-than-honest old attitudes about my moods. Normal as they are, the Object Culture tells us that no woman should ever be affected by hormone-based, emotional shifts. POWs don't suffer from cycles of bloating and impatience. I was subconsciously reluctant to admit to having these symptoms, lest I be labeled imperfect.

OPO: *Wait a minute. There's nothing bad about trying to be the best. You're not telling people to be honest—you're excusing them for failing!*

Toni: *It's just like OPO to equate being a unique, individual human being with failure. No one needs an excuse for being imperfect. It is in our natures to be imperfect, and we pay a big price when we deceive ourselves and others about this Real truth. Our imperfections and problems don't define us. Whether we can handle them honestly does.*

OPO: *Well, I think we should try to be as close to perfect as possible.*

Toni: *When it's applied to people, "perfect" is an Object, Thinglish word. It's also a moving target. Yesterday's perfect is today's has-been. We have to define the quality of life by our own standards or we will never be okay with who we really are. We will never be truly honest.*

The Trouble with Dishonesty

Scientists who study human interactions say that just about everyone lies once in a while, whether they tell a so-called white lie—"No, I really like your outfit!"—or engage in a pattern of more serious deceit. In one magazine survey of a hundred women, forty-four said they would rather be a better liar than a more honest person. The women surveyed admitted they lied about their weight, sexual history, age, salary, and education. They also said they cheated on tests, résumés, and taxes. Nearly half had lied in order to seem more desirable to a man. Lies are so commonplace in the Object Culture that in certain circumstances—during political contests, for example, or while buying a used car—we are shocked when deceptions are *not* part of the process.

While we may have different views of seemingly innocent lies, we all understand that deceiving others about serious matters is inherently wrong. We know that our lies hurt other people, and over the long run, they hurt us. Some of the most destructive lies are the ones we tell ourselves about our AS IF lives. We hide our pain, frustration, even the joy we experience in areas that aren't considered womanly. Eventually, this denial makes it hard for us to remember who we Really are. When we are dishonest about who we Really are, we don't just *tell* a lie, we turn our very lives *into* a lie. We deny others a chance to know us, and we embark on a terribly draining way of life that requires us to constantly maintain a false image.

In its simplest, most superficial form, this deception

involves an elaborate effort to make ourselves look different—usually younger, sexier, richer, and more perfect—than we are. It's done with makeup, hairstyles, clothes, and underwear that binds, pushes, and pulls us. Some women are so desperate to maintain their façades they won't be seen, even by their husbands, without all this camouflage. (One woman jokingly told me she wouldn't check her e-mail without putting on lipstick.)

Worse is the dishonesty we employ when we interact with people in ways that deny our true feelings. We lie about how we feel, what we believe, and even what we own. As a result, we have to keep track of what we said to whom and cover up all evidence that contradicts the false image we intend to project. When I think about women who have this problem, I imagine they are like the plate spinners who used to appear in variety shows. While an orchestra played "The Flight of the Bumblebee," the entertainer ran around the stage, keeping several plates spinning atop wobbly sticks. Everyone watching felt the tension build as the spinner struggled to keep the plates from falling and breaking.

Why do we put ourselves into a situation where we must anxiously maintain so many deceptions? Women who get caught up in a pattern of dishonesty are often responding to one or a series of deep-seated emotions related to their struggle to be POWs. Women who judge themselves harshly are ashamed and may lie to cover whatever flaws they imagine they have. Insecurity and anxiety can lead to lies designed to create feelings of control. The same is true when we fear that we're going to be rejected. In order to hang on to another's approval, we may even construct a false personality if we think it will please others.

In time, the dishonesty fueled by these powerful emotions can become a habit. To protect our egos, we may even try to convince ourselves that the unRealistic image we have constructed for the world is genuine. However, a false claim of happiness, backed up by a fake smile, never works. Deep down you know that you are hiding your Real self, but you have done it for so long that you may not even know who you are.

Honesty Doesn't Have to Be Brutal

In a culture obsessed with avoiding pain, where OPO tries to make us feel ashamed about our mistakes and imperfections, it's no wonder many of us are afraid of the truth, even admitting it to ourselves. Afraid of the truth, we tell ourselves the lie that this cookie, this purchase, this sexual conquest, this perfectly vacuumed rug will make us feel better. Or at least, in the short run, it will help us avoid our own internalized judgments.

It doesn't help that OPO is sometimes expressed in aggressive, even hostile forms. Too often, people who claim to speak the truth "for your own good" are actually just using their opinions to try to control us. This is why we recoil whenever someone says, "May I be brutally honest?" We know the point is mainly brutality, not honesty. Invariably, the speaker wants to give voice to hostility, anger, or aggression. (The next time someone asks this question, how about saying, "Why do you have the need to be brutal?")

Real honesty, because it is leavened with empathy, is not unkind. It is not an attack, and it is not manipulative. Real honesty has a different purpose. It is intended to give us understanding that allows for growth and change. It has nothing to do with tearing a person down. It is also essential to the development of self-empathy, accepting responsibility for our mistakes to begin to recover from shame and guilt.

Of course, such honesty is not always easy. Honesty

of every type can feel threatening. But the fear that arises with honesty can be soothed when you let go of the belief that you *must* be perfect and that you *must* feel ashamed if you have made mistakes in the past or have room for improvement.

No one is a paragon of a perfectly Real woman. We all struggle. We are, each of us, inconsistent and imperfect. It is these flaws that make us human. If you accept this truth, you can then assess yourself honestly, without fear. You can also develop the sensitivity to share your honest feelings with others, without being brutal. One good technique for practicing this type of real honesty is called "I, Not You."

If when you tell the truth you start speaking with the word *I* rather than the word *you*, there is a very good chance you will be heard and accepted. For example, instead of saying "You make me feel terrible when you ignore me," you might try "I miss you, and I want to spend more time with you." Both statements may seem to be honest, but one version lets you cast blame, while the other takes responsibility.

It can be difficult to chose the "I feel" approach. However, after you try it a few times, you will notice that others, relieved that your honesty is not brutal, respond with empathy. If you are with people you trust, you can express your emotions bravely, even the ones that make you uncomfortable. If they have true empathy for you, they will welcome the truth and admire you for saying it. They will also be more likely to join you in conversation rather than engage in conflict.

For the advanced students, the next phase in Real communication is the ever-popular "why." To employ this skill, use the following template: I feel _____ when _____ and here's why _____.

Honestly Embrace Your Contradictions

W ithout shame, we can look honestly at all aspects of our lives, and we don't have to feel bad about the contradictions we discover. Take, for example, the shame I once felt over the fact that I love to read mainstream women's magazines. Here I am, the woman who fights the Object Culture, and I enjoy leafing through pages and pages on beauty and lifestyle. I even appreciate the creativity in the advertising.

Surprised? Do you think I'm hypocritical? I understand if you do. After all, I'm the one who warns everyone about the impossible standards promoted by the mass media and urges you to resist their influence.

But what if I understand the negatives that come with these magazines and still enjoy looking through them? Should I feel ashamed and declare myself dishonest? I don't think so. If I have empathy for myself, I can recognize that a host of influences contributed to the development of my personality and character. Some of my likes and dislikes will be difficult to explain and reconcile. But as long as I am not hurting anyone—including myself—a little inconsistency is perfectly human and perfectly all right.

Every woman lives with similar, apparent inconsistencies that seem, on the face, dishonest. Maybe you are devoted to equality of the sexes, but love having doors opened for you. You value other people, but sometimes grow impatient with them. You worry about violence in our culture, but have a thing for action-hero movies. You object to the way mass media portrays women as sex objects, but like the effect certain lingerie has on your husband or partner.

When you look at yourself honestly, do you notice these kinds of paradoxes? Undoubtedly, you do. If you lie about yourself and demand that others meet a standard you cannot attain, perhaps this makes you hypocritical. But if you are honest about your foibles, and you aren't demanding that others do something different, then maybe you aren't a hypocrite at all. Maybe you are just a complex human being making her way in a world that presents infinite challenges and equally infinite possibilities. You can be honest about your choices, and you don't have to lie about them.

Secrets Can Hurt You

While much of what is covered in this chapter is lighthearted, it's important to recognize that unacknowledged emotions and loyalty to the Object Culture ideal can lead women to hide the truth in ways that can be extremely destructive. Secret drinking, drug use, eating disorders, or other problems can be indicators a woman is afraid of the truth.

One pernicious and common deception among women is compulsive shopping, which can lead to debts that dominate their lives. One woman I work with acquired several secret credit cards, which she gradually ran up to their limits. Soon, much of her life revolved around hiding this debt. New purchases were squirreled away in the attic. She ran to get the mail before her husband could so he wouldn't see the bills, and she maintained a secret checkbook. The stress of this effort was bad enough. Then she realized that she would have to postpone her dream of going back to college because she couldn't pay her bills.

As we worked together, this credit-dependent woman gradually became honest about her behavior and the hidden feelings that were behind it. For years she had refused to admit that she felt overly controlled by her husband. Once she was able to tell this truth, she could admit that the shopping was an expression of both her individuality—I can make my own decisions!—and her hostility.

Secret credit cards are remarkably common, as are secret sexual affairs and secret addictions to drugs and alcohol. In many cases, such dishonest behaviors are responses to unacknowledged feelings. Once we can be open, at least with ourselves, about destructive secret activities, we can begin to ask about the feelings behind them. I often discover that these secret activities are performed to soothe pain or to assert control. Sometimes they point to a conflict between your Real self and your daily feelings and actions.

If this is happening to you, it's time to think again about your values and beliefs, and see if your behavior is consistent with them. For example, do you say that you value relationships over money and status? Almost every woman I have ever met would claim she does. But then a great many put far more time and effort into earning and spending money and distracting themselves than they devote to caring for their Real selves and the people they love. For example, do you say you live for your kids and yet ignore them in favor of talking on the phone, using the computer, or watching TV? If you discover a similar sort of conflict in yourself, the solution isn't a descent into guilt and self-criticism, but rather a courageous recognition of the need to understand and change.

An Honesty Exercise

omen who live under the powerful influence of the Object Culture, which threatens us with shame and humiliation if we fall short of its standards, can become so accustomed to pretending that they find it difficult to be honest about how they Really feel. They are out of the habit of self-reflection, and they fear what they might hear coming from their hearts if they stopped and listened to them carefully. Some have lost the ability to ask themselves the kinds of questions that lead to the truth.

Those who need to gain access to their own honesty and get emotionally "unstuck" can benefit from a simple exercise that helps them explore something they take for granted—their own hands—with fresh, compassionate eyes.

The Hand Exercise

In a moment when you know you won't be interrupted, find a safe place where you can sit quietly, preferably at a table. Rest your hands on the table in front of you and let yourself study them, front and back, as if they are truly new to you. Now, ask yourself the following questions, and give yourself time to reflect before you answer.

How do you generally feel about your hands? *Why?*

Do you feel different about them right now? *Why?*

Do you feel the same way about both of them? *Why?*

If you could change your hands in any way, what would you change? *Why?*

What have others told you about your hands?

How often do you really look at your hands?

Do you do anything to take care of them? What do you do? How often?

Why do, or don't, you take care of your hands?

Do you wear jewelry on your hands? *Why?*

Do you wear the same jewelry every day, or do you change it? *Why?*

Where did your jewelry come from?

How do you choose what to wear?

Do you communicate anything with your jewelry?

What kinds of things do you do with your hands?

What are your favorite things to do with your hands?

Why do you enjoy these activities?

What are the least favorite things you do with your hands?

Why do you dislike these activities?

Do your hands remind you of anyone?

When you look at them, do you recall a certain time and place?

How do you feel about your hands right now?

When I did this exercise in a class, a student offered some new questions: "Who have you loved with these hands? How? Did you love enough with them?" I think they are good additions to the exercise. You may think of others.

Although it seems simple enough, the hand exercise helps us to move past anxiety, focus our minds, and see ourselves with greater truthfulness. It teaches the practice of calm reflection. It may also produce some startling results. Some people discover that their hands remind them of their parents, and they find either comfort or distress in this realization. Others develop deep appreciation for their hands in all their complexity. Some hands are strong. Some have suffered and bear scars or carry the pain of arthritis or injury. But in every hand there is a lifetime of experiences and emotions. They carry messages about who we have been, who we are, and who we hope to be.

The hand exercise will help you be more empathetically honest about yourself. If you take the same technique—slow, compassionate questioning—and apply it to other aspects of yourself, to relationships, to other people, you will get the same kind of result. Real honesty grows when you bravely explore and suspend judgment and fear, so you can get to understanding.

Honesty Doesn't Make You a Bitch

Real women who are honest with themselves and others can't help but take honesty one step further. Inevitably, they start sharing their honest feelings and opinions about all sorts of things—relationships, work, even politics—and they do it with increasing confidence and ease because they feel less intimidated by OPO and less worried about being POWs devoted to pleasing everyone else.

> OPO: *Watch out. Toni's telling you to go ahead and be a "bitch on wheels."*
> Toni: *Again with the name-calling?*

Few words have the power to silence, but "bitch" is one of them. It suggests an overly aggressive, snarling sort of woman who speaks from a well of anger with the manipulative purpose of inflicting pain. Admittedly, there are times when both women and men display this kind of behavior. But there are many moments when the term is applied unfairly. It is often used to shut people up when they want to tell their truth.

Is it bitchy to say how you feel or to express your opinions calmly and reasonably? Absolutely not. In fact, if you have strong feelings about something and close your mouth just to please others, you will develop the kind of anger and resentment that can come out as bitchy behavior. But if you are merely honest—not hostile or shaming—as you express yourself, then you can never be bitchy.

How can we practice genuine truthfulness? With empathy. When we reflect empathetically before speaking up, and then consider the emotional effects our words will have, it's easy to frame statements in a nonjudgmental and constructive way. Using this sort of Realness, empathetic honesty is especially effective with people you love and who love you back.

But in the end, if you are true to your beliefs and emotions, you will find yourself in situations where you must tell uncomfortable truths. The good news is that if you have been Real with them, the people who know you and love you will want to hear it.

Serious Truths

o discussion of honesty would be complete without reference to how truth can save our lives, bring us justice, and set us free. This Real fact was impressed on me by a mother who corresponded with me via the Velveteen Principles website.

Elena had married a man who turned out to be distant, controlling, and temperamental. When she became depressed, she entered psychotherapy and struggled to recall her own childhood. (She was one of those people who didn't seem to have any memories of herself at a young age.) In sessions with her therapist, Elena repeatedly said she felt suspicious about her husband, but she couldn't say why.

As so often happens, a child led the mother to the truth. In a moment when they seemed to be fighting about some teenage acting out, Elena's daughter shouted that her father had molested her. In a moment, the pieces of the puzzle clicked together. Elena's suspicions were based on her fear that her husband was a sexual predator. Her daughter's statement broke Elena's denial.

Remarkably, Elena's husband actually confessed

what he had done and accepted a divorce. (Elena couldn't bring herself to file criminal charges against him, but denied him visitation.) In therapy, Elena eventually let herself recall that she had been sexually abused as a girl by a neighbor. She came to understand that her subconscious effort to block that memory had also blotted out all recollections of her childhood.

When the truth crashed down on Elena, it did create a crisis and caused her great pain. But it also allowed her to take some heroic actions. She dropped her denial about what was happening in her home, confronted a predator who had harmed her child, and became honest about her own life. The shame that once kept her silent was replaced by pride about finally standing up for herself and her daughter.

Velveteen

Principle #7

Real Women Are Generous

When sons and daughters grow up and leave home to make their own way in the world, their parents, mothers especially, feel the loss. After my client Mary Anne sent her daughter, Janice, away to college, she had trouble identifying her feelings clearly or saying what she missed the most. Then Janice called to say she wanted to come to see Mary Anne for a few days to be fed, talk things over, and collect some hugs. The next time I met with Mary Anne, she was happy, and she knew precisely what she had missed most about having her daughter nearby.

"When she asked to come home and told me what she needed, it felt so good because I knew that I could give it to her," she told me excitedly. "I realized that what I missed most was giving to her, taking care of her, and feeling like I was doing it right."

Indeed, what Janice had done for Mary Anne was a wonderful gift. She gave her mother a chance to be generous. This is because Real women, all people actually, feel good when they have a chance to be generous. It's even better when an opportunity arises that is so clear and unambiguous that we don't have to worry about getting it wrong or messing it up, and then feeling embarrassed or ashamed.

When you are Real and you operate from a base of courage and honesty, it's easier to overcome the fear that holds people back and prevents them from being generous. Real women look for and find lots of opportunities to give in a variety of ways—emotionally, financially, intellectually, spiritually. The ultimate act of generosity involves giving others our love, and when we do that, we actually help them to become a little more Real, too. This is the message conveyed by the Fairy in *The Velveteen Rabbit*:

"Wasn't I Real before?" asked the little Rabbit.

"You were Real to the Boy," the Fairy said, "because he loved you. Now you shall be Real to everyone."

In Margery Williams's story, love, generously offered, is so powerful that it helps the little bunny achieve his life's dream. It transforms him from sawdust and cloth into a Real rabbit with a twitching nose. Of course, in the Object Culture, where Real is discouraged, generosity doesn't flow as freely as it might in the nursery in the story. Obstacles to giving are everywhere, and we have to learn about them and learn how to overcome them if we are going to live as Real women.

Generosity Toward Others in a Competitive World

Sylvia is one of the most magazine-perfect women I have ever met. Although she's approaching forty, she could pass for thirty. She has big, wide-set eyes, high cheekbones, and a slim body. Her dark hair is so thick and shiny that she could pose for a shampoo ad. Her skin is clear, soft, and radiant.

By the standards of the Object Culture, Sylvia is the Perfect Object Woman and should be reaping the benefits. In fact, she receives more snide comments than admiration, especially from other women who think that Sylvia "has it all" and doesn't need their consideration—or their generosity.

"On a day when I'm not wearing makeup, people ask, 'What's wrong with you? Are you sick?'" explains Sylvia. "On the days when I do wear makeup, they say, 'Well, you look beautiful, as usual,' as if they are annoyed." No one, male or female, seems interested in what Sylvia thinks or feels or even considers that there's anything important to know about her. She's beautiful, so they assume she's got it made.

That's the problem. In the Object Culture, we're all constantly comparing and competing with one another. Some members of Twelve Step groups call this the "compare and despair" dynamic because even when you win, the effect is negative. Your victory separates you from others.

As a superior object, Sylvia is often regarded as a "winner." What others don't see is that Sylvia must deal with the same problems and heartaches all of us confront—illness, job stress, the challenges of family, and financial problems. "Sometimes I think I have to make myself less attractive to be taken seriously. But then I think that wouldn't work either. And besides, if I don't have my looks, I don't have anything."

Just like Nickel the sea turtle, Sylvia's appearance didn't tell the whole story. Throughout her childhood she had been the victim of a sadistic father who told her she was good for one thing—sex. As an adult, she lives in constant conflict over her beauty and how others perceive her. Sylvia's experience may be more severe than others because she is subject to considerable jealousy and resentment. However, we have all felt what she feels— that too often people don't even try to get to know us. Instead they evaluate us, determine our apparent status— is it high or low?—and then figure out how to relate to us.

The terrible irony in this process is that the status symbols we are urged to acquire and show off with great flair often alienate others and make them less likely to approach us generously. An enormous car with tinted windows separates us from other drivers and people on the street. An exclusive address behind locked gates can ward off people we might want to know. You may know that your armful of expensive jewelry recalls the love behind each piece; others may see it as a reminder of what they do not own themselves.

The Object Culture trains us to study status signals with great care. (One advertisement, for example, says:

"It's your watch that tells most about who you are.") Knowing that others observe us closely, we have to be careful about the signals we send, understanding that if we try to set ourselves above others, we also set ourselves apart from them.

Many who meet her are unable to get past Sylvia's appearance and focus on her as a person. Unfortunately, she can't either. For her own protection, she also tends to adopt a detached attitude. For these reasons, Sylvia rarely receives a kind word or consideration from the people she meets.

But, of course, beauty isn't the only superficial quality that seems to stop us from being generous with each other. We reject each other for being too thin or too fat, too rich or too poor, too loud or too quiet, too smart or too slow. The possibilities are so great that it seems like people just look for a reason to turn away from one another. In fact, we do it all the time.

We cannot be generous because we are so busy striving and achieving and feeling inadequate. And because acquisitions in the Object Culture are supposedly in short supply, we must desperately guard what we have for fear of losing it. We feel at once anxiously urgent and at a loss in a culture of competitiveness. Before the communication/media age, we could only compare ourselves to others in our community. Now we have access to the entire international scene filled with superstars, supermodels, and superachievers. I am not immune to this self-defeating process. Sometimes I wonder if I'm smart enough to even write this book. I compare myself to the great women writers, women whose work affected me deeply, and I come up short in my own mind. In these moments of doubt, when I'm almost paralyzed by anxiety, OPO often speaks to me from within:

OPO: *Who do you think you are? What can you say that hasn't been said before?*
Toni: *I know this is just the culture of competitiveness talking. The world is a big place, OPO. There's room in it for my voice and my book. And I don't have to compete. I just have to be Real.*

The idea that there is room for all of us and our creations is a radical challenge to the mainstream notion that everyone is either a "winner" or a "loser." But if we don't have faith in the idea of a generous world, we're condemned to adopt a scarcity mentality that makes us so worried about ourselves that we cannot think of others. Instead of being open and generous, we are tight, guarded, and withholding. We cannot get past our own fears and anxieties even to consider giving of ourselves. This is especially true in two important areas of life: work and love.

Have you noticed that women have trouble supporting each other at work? In part this is due to a history of inequality between the sexes. A woman who already fears her opportunities are more limited than a man's may be reluctant to help other women on the job. But this competitiveness doesn't seem to diminish when conditions improve. I've noticed that even when female bosses run a workplace, insecurity still runs high, and spontaneous generosity is in short supply.

Equally troubling is the competition among women for mates. Driven by the need for security and status, women can be particularly hard on each other when winning a potential husband or partner. Many women even withhold their support when a friend finds love before they do. For the woman who feels alone, her fear, anxiety, and self-doubt—Am I a good enough Object? —may overwhelm her ability to be caring and generous.

Life Is Not a Competition

One of the big lies of the Object Culture holds that in reaching certain goals—a perfect mate, home, family, and possessions—you'll find fulfillment. As Sylvia knows, superficial achievements, especially those that are the result of genetic advantages, actually leave you with an empty heart yearning to connect with others. The trouble is that empty hearts have nothing to give. They lack generosity of spirit.

Filling an empty heart begins when you shift your focus from Object Culture competitiveness to a self-directed life. When you adjust your purpose and seek positive relationships, meaningful work, and outlets for your creativity and passions, your prospects for happiness improve automatically, and your heart is soon enriched.

A good example can be seen in how Real women approach work. At my neighborhood diner, I always try to get a table in the section shepherded by a sixty-something woman named Bette. There is nothing glamorous about Bette's job, and she's certainly not going to get rich doing it. But she mothers every customer, obviously taking pleasure in feeding their stomachs and warming their hearts with her smile.

Bette opted out of the great Object competition years ago. She chose to be her Real self, and she projects her values—she likes good people, good humor, and good food—with courage and honesty. I've watched Bette mentor new waitresses and show genuine concern for her customers. She is better for it because every day she benefits from teamwork with her coworkers, and her tips include hundreds of smiles and jokes and kind words. Filled up by these responses, Bette is able to give even more generously.

Away from work, a generous, noncompetitive approach to relationships can make the difference between a broken heart and a full one. Unfortunately, the life-is-a-contest message that pulses throughout the Object Culture affects friendships, relations between neighbors, even marriages. I know husbands and wives who compete over their salaries, physical appearances, and even who's the favorite parent.

In every case, competition in relationships can be destructive, but perhaps the most painful cases involve siblings. It is not surprising that some of the oldest stories in human history, from the Old Testament to ancient myths, revolve around brothers and sisters. The seeds of competitiveness can be planted very early in these relationships as children vie for attention. Parents can try to ease this conflict and may even actively discourage it, but sometimes it can be impossible to avoid.

I've seen in my counseling work that some of women's deepest wounds are inflicted by their sisters. It is all too common for sisters to judge each other, to compete against each other, and to harbor longstanding hurt feelings. I have listened to many women talk about which sister in a family is "the pretty one" or "the smart one" or "the rebellious one."

These are, of course, Thinglish terms. In every case, the label barely describes the woman who carries it. Instead it creates a barrier that makes it impossible for people who grew up together and could be the closest of friends to have the relationship they desire.

The scarcity mentality and Object values are almost always at the root of sister conflicts. In childhood, girls who feared that there wasn't enough love in their family for everyone learn to resent a sibling's apparent advantages of beauty, intelligence, talent, and even luck. In adolescence, these feelings can grow more intense if one girl gets a lot of attention and another does not. Later in life, adult women who judge themselves negatively because they fail to meet impossible standards turn the same harsh light on their sisters. They may feel momentarily better if they cut a sibling "down to size," but the relief doesn't last long. Soon it is replaced by shame, grief over what is lost, and a longing for connection.

You may have noticed that alienated sisters often repair their relationship in midlife, after they realize that no one ever wins all the supposed rewards promised by the Object Culture. This makes sense. It's much easier to drop out of the competition when you finally see that it's rigged. Then you have the time and energy to set your own priorities and move toward them.

In Real relationships, competition, which must yield a winner and a loser, is replaced with negotiation, compromise, and (sometimes) agreeing to disagree in an empathetic way. This way of getting along becomes easier when winning and losing are no longer options. But reconciliation doesn't make up for lost years. For this reason, I urge sisters in conflict to get Real as soon as possible. Courage, honesty, and empathy (for yourself and others) will let you see others, including your sister, with new generosity. Of course, it's possible that she hasn't let go of the scarcity mentality and remains snared in the Object Culture, but that can't stop you from loving her, and yourself, better right now.

Practicing Generosity with Yourself

As with most of the Velveteen Principles, the practice of Real generosity starts with yourself, which some people assume means a whole lot of shopping or pampering at a spa or fancy meals and vacations. It's possible that these are ways that you can be generous with yourself, but before you rush out to indulge in generic self-care, think about your past experiences with gifts.

Most of the women I know could fill a closet, or at least a kitchen cupboard, with things they have received from people who seemed to put little or no thought into their gift choices. Valentine's Day brings a box of chocolates and a store-bought card. A birthday equals jewelry. For winter holidays it's a robe and slippers. Technically, these are fine presents. But when they come from the people who love us and know us best, they can be a little disappointing because they are generic.

Granted, gift giving can be a challenging and emotional task. If you're giving something to a committed citizen of the U.S. of G., for example, it's likely they find generic gifts easiest to accept. And sometimes people are so anxious to please that they don't think clearly and must fall back on generic ideas. We love these gifts anyway, as well as the people who give them. But aren't we happier when someone understands the difference between pleasing us and being truly generous by matching their choice of a present with our unique values and passions?

We like receiving gifts that show someone else thought about us and knows us. Even if someone has to ask us for help, that's better than a generic effort. For example, one of my clients surprised her husband when she said she really wanted a basketball hoop instead of jewelry or clothes. He got her one, and it is one of her favorite things in the world.

One of my favorite gifts came from my daughter who found a piece of "junque" furniture at the curb and brought it to me. She arrived home exhausted from dragging it up the road, but she was also elated. She knew this was a perfect gift for me. She also experienced the pleasant feeling that comes with true generosity, which is based on thought and effort, not the amount we spend on a gift.

When we decide to be generous with ourselves—to care for ourselves—we can shirk the generic and be particular. We can move beyond getting our hair and nails done or buying a new pair of shoes, and be specific about acts or objects of generosity that nurture our inner, Real selves.

If you want to practice Real self-care, start by reconsidering how you talk to yourself. Every day we conduct an inner dialogue—thinking about decisions, experiences, problems, relationships—that both reflects and contributes to our moods. For many women, this conversation is a matter of harsh judgments and reprimands. Echoing the values of the Object Culture, or some internalized scold, they heap criticisms and scorn on themselves:

How could you be so stupid?
You'll never be good enough.
Don't you ever learn?
You are so fat.
You aren't athletic like your sister.
You are the black sheep of the family.

These generalities cover many of the themes that echo in women's minds, but, of course, we all express them in unique ways. One woman I work with described her thoughts that come after she eats potato chips (one of her favorite indulgences): "I am disgusting. I need to shower so I don't smell gross. Who does this—eating chips alone? Pathetic. Now hide the bag so no one will know what a pig you are. Not in the kitchen trash, but in the can outside, so no one will know who ate them."

If this kind of self-talk seems familiar, it's time to give yourself a break and practice a little self-empathy by recognizing your own struggles, the history that brought you to where you are now, and the progress you have already made toward your life's goals. Try replacing the scolder who dwells inside you (the one who judges you a loser) with the voice of a kind and generous parent. If you never had the kind of mother or father who understood your failings and encouraged you, it's time to do it for yourself. Who else is going to tell you that you don't have to be perfect in order to be worthy? Who else is going to tell you to go ahead and pursue your hopes and dreams?

Tending to your passions is the ultimate form of generous self-care. For one woman I know, this has meant devotion to preserving historic buildings in her community. A lover of history, Irene never thought of herself as an activist. But then she gave herself permission to read up on her town's rich past. She joined the local historical society and got involved in preservation projects. At first glance, this may not fit your idea of generous "self-care." But, in fact, Irene was making her own interest a priority and giving herself time to pursue it. The reward was deeper enjoyment of history, connections with others at the historical society, and the satisfaction of contributing to her community.

Your self-care strategies can be as distinctive as Irene's. Maybe you always wanted to write a memoir. Classes on writing can be found in every community. Why not enroll, then give yourself the gift of time to develop a manuscript? Or maybe you need to take care of yourself in a bigger way.

Self-care requires that we be Really honest about our particular interests, values, and beliefs. This is even truer when we think about our lives beyond hobbies or casual concerns. Far too many women sacrifice essential parts of themselves in the pursuit of Object goals, such as the perfect relationship, the perfect family, or the perfect body. When they eventually realize what they have lost, these women may feel that it is too late to go after certain things, like an education, a job, or a profession. It is almost never too late. A good friend of mine attended classes at Harvard University, no less, at age ninety-two. She was concerned about attending seminars with a walker, but she went anyway. She acted out of respect for her own Real values and the firm belief that she deserved to learn and grow.

Being Generous with Others

At the end of the school year, many teachers find little piles of thank-you gifts on their desks. Many have a red apple theme: plastic red apples to hold candy, ceramic red apples filled with paperclips, notepads decorated with little drawings of red apples. Like chocolate at Valentine's Day, the red apple gifts do not make a lasting impression. But there are gifts that teachers treasure forever. Most are notes, letters, and handmade cards that carry heartfelt messages. They say, "Thank you for teaching me how to multiply fractions," or "You helped my child," or "I learned a lot from you." These presents remind a teacher of her value as a person. They affirm her choice to become an educator, and they reward her with genuine emotion.

When we no longer feel driven to be competitive, and we understand that life offers enough rewards for everyone to feel secure and safe, it's possible to reach out to others with a specific and honest kind of generosity. The gifts we give encourage their passions. More important, we offer our time, experience, and wisdom if we have it in a way that is not judgmental, threatening, or competitive. Whenever I see an accomplished person encourage another's progress, I am reminded of the wonderful statement Mark Twain made on this subject: "Keep away from people who belittle your ambitions. Small people always do that, but the really great make you feel that you too can become great."

Opportunities for generous encouragement appear in many settings. In our day-to-day lives, we get the chance to smile at someone, offer a compliment, share a bit of conversation. In one class I teach, we do an exercise that requires each student to write down something positive about each person in the class. I know that these notes are appreciated and in some cases are cherished for years. Similar opportunities to be generous abound. Why can't women be generous with each other, lift each other up, and applaud each other's efforts and passions in the same way that we compliment nice clothes and jewelry? Certainly all of us who have reached middle age can generously mentor a younger or less experienced woman who shares our passion for a career or other interest.

One of the most influential people in my early life was my French teacher, Madame Diaz. She probably had no idea how significant she was to me. We never had any intense heart-to-heart talks about my troubled home situation, and I knew nothing about her personal life. But she was generous enough to treat me with respect, as though I was worth something, at a time when I needed it. I thought, *If this woman, whom I respect, respects me, then maybe I can be okay.* Thanks, Madame Diaz, wherever you are.

Life offers us endless opportunities to be generous. Some of the most obvious occur when people turn to us when illness, death, or other forms of tragedy strike, and we discover the depths of our strength and generosity. Real women have great inner resources we can draw upon. We can remind people that material things are temporary. The Object Culture cannot define our happiness. Our inner, Real selves are always beautiful.

This last kind of generosity—sharing our strength in a time of need—is actually something women do very well. Studies have shown that we tend to draw closer to people who require help, while men tend to shy away. But we don't have to wait for hard times to give of ourselves. Sometimes the most generous thing we can do is simply to listen to another person. She may have sorrow or joy to express. She may ask for our advice or need us to simply affirm her feelings. If you can provide just what she wants, nothing more and nothing less, you will perform an act of true generosity.

I have little doubt that you have practiced Real generosity already. It comes quite naturally once you have adopted a Real perspective, become more empathetic, and begun to move through your world with more courage and honesty. For this reason, I don't need to tell you that generosity creates a "feedback loop." But this point is worth a reminder. Every time you give of yourself and touch another person in a direct and specific way, you receive in return Real nourishment—gratitude, connection, and encouragement. Generosity leads to generosity, and it reinforces what is Real in you.

The Generosity Inventory

Generosity, like courage, honesty, and other important aspects of character, is not something we think about on a regular basis. If you want to recall your own experience with generosity, identify your attitudes toward it, and cultivate the generosity impulse, consider sitting down with pen and paper and making a generosity inventory by answering these questions:

How was giving practiced in my family?

Was there a scarcity mentality in my home, or did people believe there was "enough" for everyone?

Was anyone especially generous to me—giving time, wisdom, material things—and how did this giving affect me?

Who wasn't generous in these ways?

Am I generous with myself? If I am, how do I practice self-generosity? If I am not generous with myself, why not?

Do I compete and compare when it comes to generosity?

Do I judge myself harshly?

What do I most want to receive from others?

What do I most want to give?

What's holding me back from being as generous as I want to be?

As you take your generosity inventory, allow yourself to ask more questions and develop answers that are as deep and complex as possible. Don't forget to ask why. Give yourself permission to explore the subject without criticizing yourself or letting OPO stop you. When you are finished, reflect on your answers and consider whether they point to ways that you can give more to yourself and others. I bet they do.

Velveteen

Principle #8

Real Women Are Grateful

Have you noticed by now that I am a worrier? In my Bag of Rocks, I have stones labeled "anxious" and "high-strung" and "extra-vigilant." I collected these rocks during an insecure childhood, when everything from family finances to my physical safety was in doubt.

As an adult I recognized the source of my tendency to worry, but understanding it didn't fully eliminate it. Every once in a while I find myself anxiously considering the family budget and getting lost in worries. At other moments I wonder if I have done enough as a parent or tried hard enough in my work. When I notice I'm stuck in this kind of unproductive and self-doubting thought, I find an antidote in one single word: gratitude.

Nothing has helped me to recognize the Real wonders in the world around me, the value of the people I love, and the progress I have made in my own life more than the practice of simple gratitude. When I give myself permission to look at life through grateful eyes, I discover an almost endless number of sources of Real happiness, including the following:

Relationships with my husband, daughters, friends, colleagues, clients, and others

Pleasures, such as good food, music, films, books, and activities

Environments, including my home and its gardens, my community, and places while traveling

Ideas that I discover in my work and in my striving to be more Real

Feelings that guide me to what is most Real and positive in life

All of these things and more inspire me to feel grateful. But in a world where competition is the norm and things are used to measure happiness, gratitude doesn't always come easily. Fear and self-doubt can obscure the positive parts of life and even cause us to forget how to be grateful.

In the United States of Generica, we are bombarded with media messages about how we should look, what we should buy, and how we should live. These messages are crafted to make us feel frustrated and inadequate. The effect is like living with an insecure and angry adolescent—one who is full of judgment and condemnation—inside your head.

At the same time, many of our encounters with other people involve subtle and not so subtle competitions over status. We hear another woman's news about her kids on the honor roll, a new job, or a move to a big house, and we wonder if we are keeping up.

These encounters and the media barrage have a truly corrosive effect on how we think about ourselves. A good example is a young friend of mine named Vicky who was remarkably successful in school and upon graduation immediately found a job in her field. She had good friends, a lovely apartment, and was adjusting well to a new city, but whenever she thought about her life, she focused relentlessly on the one thing that wasn't perfect: her uneven experience with love and romance.

"It's like I measure everything in my life as a bar graph," Vicky explained to me. "There are bars for all these things like friendship, creativity, satisfying work, my home. They are all represented by really tall bars, near the top of the chart. But there's that bad one that's low, and I wind up thinking about it all the time."

Most of us focus on the one or two "low bars" on our charts. The alternative attitude is seemingly simple: gratitude for all those elevated bars, which represent who you are, what you have, and how you live right now. If you focus intently on how well you are doing in so many areas of your life, then your dissatisfaction, worry, and anxieties will recede. You will also find it easier to live in the moment (to really absorb what you are reading this very moment, for example) instead of dwelling on regret about the past or fear of the future.

I say that this practice is *seemingly* simple because gratitude does not come naturally to most of us who live in the United States of Generica. Here, where very few of us have a reasonable sense of when we have "enough," dissatisfaction is the norm, and fighting it with gratitude is an act of defiance.

Be a Revolutionary

Today, the practice of gratitude is sometimes considered a rebellious act. You must be willing to challenge Object Culture assumptions, often taking a position that is the exact opposite of the majority view. Because body image is such an enormous issue for women (and a source of almost universal pain), it's perfect for an illustration of how your rebellion might unfold. It involves making a conscious choice and effort to defy mainstream thinking and reframe how we think about our bodies. Here are some examples of Object thinking about the body and grateful alternatives:

	Object Thinking	Grateful Alternatives
My whole body	Fat, skinny, short, tall, old, weak	Life-giving, sensual, loyal, expressive, blameless, a gift, ever-present
My face	Lined, blemished, asymmetrical, splotchy, disproportioned	Unique, expressive, genuine, Real, receptive
My legs	Jiggly, bony, veiny, knobby, scarred, shapeless	Useful (for balance, walking, stability, strength), supportive, valuable
My breasts	Too big, too small, saggy, pointy, mismatched, stretch-marked	Shapely (whatever shape they are), sensual, nourishing

	Object Thinking	Grateful Alternatives
My abdomen	Bloated, weak, paunchy	Feminine, female, functional, fertile
My butt	Too large, small, bony, flabby, saggy	Attractive, supportive, cute, cushioning, muscular

Your individual assessment will be unique. Disability, fertility problems, and other differences require us to think carefully about our physical selves. However, there is no body on Earth, and no body part, that deserves to be rejected and disdained. The Object Culture fetishizes supposedly perfect examples of human anatomy. But these images are unrealistic and irrelevant (not to mention airbrushed and computer enhanced). We each live in our own unique skin and are privileged to experience the world through our bodies.

I am reminded of this truth whenever I meet a woman who has dealt with a crisis like breast cancer and recovered feeling grateful to be alive. One, who underwent a double mastectomy, got a magnificent tattoo of a garden in bloom—an image of growth and beauty—across her scarred chest. No doubt she appreciates her still-beating heart now more than she ever appreciated her breasts.

Our bodies are not the only things we might appreciate more deeply. If you are rebellious enough to reject the constant striving that characterizes today's life, you'll feel grateful for things other people overlook. An old car that still gets you where you need to go is a wonder. A dated sweater that still keeps you warm is comforting. A small home may not impress like a mansion would, but aren't you grateful for the shelter on a stormy day? I know that every time it rains, I am filled with gratitude for the roof over my head. (The sound of the drops hitting it warms my heart.)

OPO: *What a cliché. The rain on the roof makes you feel good. Someday that roof will need replacing. How will you pay for it?*

Toni: *Some things are clichés because they are true. And if the roof ever leaks, I'll fix it. In the meantime, I choose gratitude. If you think I'm a simple-minded fool, so be it. But does your pessimism make you happy?*

OPO is so busy checking, comparing, and looking for problems that she cannot take pleasure in everyday life.

Gratitude for all the daily blessings you receive can drain the dissatisfaction right out of your life and make you feel more fulfilled and content. You can make gratitude a habit by training yourself to notice everything, including all the "little" things that already make your life a unique and self-designed work of art. My own list includes silly conversations with my daughters, meaningful work I choose to do, gardening, making art from found stuff. Make a list yourself, and consult it on a regular basis. You will notice that there's already more "you" in your life than you thought.

Intent vs. Outcome

When my children were young and I had begun to work some nights as a therapist, their father became a midweek family chef. The results were mixed. Macaroni and cheese and hot dogs worked out well. But the girls were horrified by his attempts at corned beef and an odd menu he called "toaster dinner," which was composed entirely of frozen items warmed in the toaster oven.

When they came to me with their complaints, our conversation moved from a focus on content—this food is bad—to process. Being naturally empathic, as most children are, they quickly agreed that their father's attempts at kid-friendly meals were sincere and heartfelt. He was not yet an able cook, but he was trying. We introduced a system of substitutions—a child-made sandwich option—that guaranteed they always had something edible at suppertime. And forevermore, my girls offered a genuine "thank you for cooking" whenever their dad put something on the table. They were grateful, if not for the specific dish, for the loving effort.

The important thing about toaster dinners and my husband's other strange meals (have you ever heard of hamdogs?) was appreciating the chef's intent, if not the outcome of the effort. This is not always easy. How many times have you left a social encounter wondering, *How could she say something so clumsy?* How many times have you unwrapped a gift and then thought, *Does he even know me?*

In most cases it is possible to separate the intent, or the idea behind an action, and its outcome. Of course, there are times when people communicate anger, hostility, and judgment. But there are many more times when you can reconsider a certain encounter or even ask about another person's intentions and discover something positive. This is often the case when sensitive women mix with socially clumsy men. Communication between the two sexes can be difficult, but it's possible to ascertain where his heart is. Recognizing another person's good intentions can change your hurt into gratitude. And even if you misinterpret someone's intent as benevolent when it isn't, you're still better off. Who would you rather be: the person who imagines the worst, or the person who imagines the best? Optimists tend to be happier, less isolated than pessimists.

A Grateful Perspective

A longtime therapy client once started her first session of a new year with a rant about the twelve months that had just passed. Her father had died. She was forced to put a beloved cat to sleep. All Eleanor felt when she looked back on the previous year was pain.

When Eleanor finished her harangue and we sat together in silence, her face softened as she began to recognize what she had overlooked. Her very small daughter had grown a year older, and Eleanor had enjoyed countless happy moments watching this little girl explore, discover, and develop. In the same period, she had enjoyed the love and support of a husband who is a very decent fellow and seems to grow more considerate and empathetic all the time.

Recognizing all these positives helped Eleanor to feel less victimized and less subject to the whims of fate, and more optimistic and grateful. All she needed to acknowledge this balance was a quiet moment to reflect and the willingness to do so. Some people seem to understand this need instinctively. In many religious traditions, the "day of rest," held to be sacred, allows believers to enjoy a weekly dose of similar reflection. In our busy modern world, this day for slowing down and reflecting is easily lost to chores, shopping, even work. It is something we must remember to give ourselves as a matter of self-care and in order to restore our strength and perspective. It's hard to have empathy, show gratitude, and be generous when you are engaged in the exhausting and frenzied pursuit of POW status.

If you need proof that time for quiet reflection helps us to be grateful for the smallest things in life, consider the last time you (or someone you cared about) were sick and bedridden. A very close friend of mine, Marina, recently spent weeks in the hospital. Too sick to focus on the distractions that normally fill our time—TV, telephone, radio, gossip—she spent hours with her eyes closed, thinking or dreamily looking out the window of her hospital room. When Marina was well enough to sit up, take food and drink, and talk, she expressed gratitude for the budding trees outside her window (it was spring), for the voices of her caregivers and loved ones, for the simple pleasure of drinking cold water.

Before she was sick, simple gratitude had not been Marina's strength. She was actually the kind of person who was more likely to see the problems in the Object Culture and speak out about them. She still enjoys debunking the myths of the U.S. of G., and she is an outspoken critic of the forces that push us to become POWs. But illness opened Marina's eyes to the good things in life and made her more grateful for them. She's grateful every day to be strong and healthy enough to take care of herself and to be able to connect with the ones she loves. She's even grateful for the job she goes to every day, even if it does require her to squeeze into pantyhose every morning and to put up with a little boredom and frustration.

Marina's gratitude, even for little things she once took for granted, depends in part on the fact that she had experienced two realities—life before illness and life afterward—that she could contrast in her mind. This experience was a mirror image of the Velveteen Rabbit's life. He had longed to be Real and suffered because he was not. When the moment finally came and he was transformed, "He gave one leap and the joy of using those hind legs was so great that he went springing about the turf. . . ." Having known life without its simple pleasures, the Rabbit was overwhelmed with happiness when he finally gained it. Having known sickness and the loss of ordinary things when she was hospitalized, Marina recognized them with joy when she got them back.

In these pages, and as you go through your life, you will see many examples of how society affects us negatively. Women do face certain prejudices and injustices. It's not fair that we're all supposed to look like supermodels, care for our children like supermoms, work for lower pay, and behave in the bedroom like porn stars. At the same time, as women we have wonderful strengths and opportunities that offer benefits every day. Caregiving, which falls to us more often than not, brings intimate connection to others. Few things in life make you feel more useful and more connected to others—as long as it's balanced with self-care.

Women are also permitted in our culture to have richer and more expressive emotional lives than men. We grow up knowing how to identify our feelings, express them, and be guided by them. We are permitted to give and accept love of all kinds more openly.

Genetics has offered women a few advantages, too. Our longer lifespan is well-established. But did you know that women are naturally better than men at language? We are also superior when it comes to manual dexterity, and our brains are better equipped to juggle several tasks at once.

Finally, women can be grateful for each other. Yes, we compete and sometimes put each other down, but a powerful support is in our friendships, too. We comfort and truly listen to each other, and we plot strategies together. Mothers share invaluable insights into child rearing. Married women coach newlyweds on the mysteries of the male psyche. In fact, the kind of support women provide for each other is so valuable and profound that it is even the subject of extensive scientific studies. Researchers have found that women's friendships contribute to lower blood pressure, increased immunity to disease, and faster recovery from illness. Of course, you don't need scientific proof to make you feel grateful for your women friends.

Just think about the times when you reached out to another woman to get advice, counsel, reassurance, or affirmation. Add the laugh-till-you-cry moments and celebrations of major milestones. Now, aren't you grateful for all the benefits that come with being a Real woman?

Be Grateful Anyway

Humorist Erma Bombeck said that children need love the most when they deserve it the least. Her meaning is clear to anyone who has ever had, or been, a child.

The same thing can be said about gratitude. Sometimes we need to summon it, even when we think there's nothing to be grateful about. In fact, there are many times when our feelings suggest a certain response— frustration, anger, self-pity—but we'll be helped most by further reflection that leads us to a much different place. The "be grateful anyway" exercise is one way to cultivate this kind of creative, even counter-intuitive, response and turn a potentially negative moment into a positive one.

I tried it recently when I was driving to work in the rain, in heavy traffic, and running late. I began to grumble to myself about the kinds of things we typically grumble about—being overworked, underpaid, under-appreciated, stressed out. On that morning as I made slow progress in my old car, I felt a headache brewing, and even my pants seemed too tight.

Then I remembered to be grateful anyway. It's a paradoxical response to high-stress moments, I know. But when I changed my focus to gratitude, still in the midst of that commute to work, things changed. No, *I* changed. I realized that my old car was still comfort-able and reliable. I was dry and safe. Suddenly, I be-came aware that I liked the color of my raincoat. I looked down at my hands and liked them. My wedding ring reminded me of Michael, who is my friend as well as my husband, and on whom I can always rely. I remembered that I like the kind of work I do. Being grateful helps make me Real.

The rest of my trip was filled with noticing the things I liked. The things I didn't like didn't disappear, but their size and impact on my mood were reduced considerably. And because I arrived at my workplace feeling balanced and positive, I could even address the challenges at work more productively. I hope you'll try this one. It really works for me, often, and in the worst moments.

Be Grateful Anyway

In a moment of stress, make yourself stop for a minute. Wherever you are, whatever you're doing, just stop and focus on where and who you are right now. Let yourself reflect on the most basic elements of your life and of yourself. Let yourself realize how much about you is good.

Start with your body. Are you feeling well physically?

Do your parts all work? If not, how many parts of you are still functioning to keep you alive?

Are you clean?

Are your clothes protecting you from the weather and helping you feel comfortable?

Are your senses, or at least some of them, attuned and working?

What do you see and hear that you like? Colors, shapes, sounds?

Have you eaten today? Did you enjoy it, and is your belly satisfied? Do you have access to food on a daily basis?

How about your home—is it comfortable, safe?

Notice all the things in your life that you like. It's so simple. But how often do you stop to be grateful anyway?

Velveteen

Principle #9

Real Women Experience Pain

Some time around age fifty, most women begin to feel an emotional pain that begins in a vague way. It's an emptiness paired with restlessness that can evolve into some really lousy moods. Having committed myself to the idea of being Real, I tried to be honest about these feelings when they came to me, and I looked for their source.

For me, the blues seem to be about my daughters becoming adults—a very necessary and positive development for them—and thereby losing a major focus in my daily life. My pain was a signal of the grief I felt over their moving away from me. It also alerted me to the fact that the focus of my identity was shifting. I was no longer required to spend so much time playing the sometimes-objectifying role of "mother."

My feelings—mostly loneliness and a bit of confusion —were also an invitation to think about a positive response. This is one of the positive elements of emotional pain—whether it arises at age fifty or occurs later or earlier or both in a woman's life. Like physical hurts, which alert us to troubles in our bodies that must be addressed, painful feelings call on us to attend to a problem in our inner selves or our relationships. If we can courageously confront its source, pain always leads us to growth.

In the case of my own empty-nest syndrome, pain led me to consider a wonderful variety of choices I could make about my future. Without all the distractions that come with being a busy mother, I had been given time and energy to think about my own deferred dreams, interests, and passions. It was time for me to become more Real, and every day that I ignored the call, I felt a little more emotional pain.

Similar pain is familiar to women of every age who become Real. It might come when we are young and beginning adult life. It can arise during a midlife health crisis or when a relationship ends. It is the pain that comes when it's time for us to stretch further toward becoming Real. It is the feeling we experience when we become open to long-suppressed passions, dreams, and desires, which we denied in our previous attempts to be Perfect Object Women.

The Myth of Total Happiness

Before we explore the painful parts of becoming Real, I would like to dispel the myth of the totally happy woman. You know who I am talking about. She's the ever-smiling, ever-charming woman who looks like she has all the Object Culture prescribes for happiness, and with every word and gesture, she tries to communicate that she is leading a pain-free life. In her eyes, however, we can see the fear and anxiety that suggest her claim isn't true. But she seems so brittle and vulnerable that we don't dare probe too deeply.

I often encounter these women at the college where I teach. One I'll always remember was a woman named Jean, who arrived for a meeting with her hair, clothes, and makeup in perfect condition and an electronic personal assistant ready to take notes and keep her on schedule. Jean was a mother, a Girl Scout leader, and a devoted wife to a disabled husband. But she assured me she was ready to earn a college degree and make a new career for herself. Jean kept to her promise for a few months, but then missed some appointments due to back pain. When weeks of illness became months, she received a leave of absence.

Jean had almost disappeared from my mind when she showed up at my office three years later. She was wearing blue jeans, a T-shirt, and barely any makeup. She told me that during her leave she had become addicted to the painkillers prescribed for her back. Through rehabilitation and counseling, she had been able to drop the "perfectly happy" façade and had begun to face a lifetime of pain, from abuse in her childhood to the grief of her husband's chronic illness. (The back pain was mostly psychosomatic, her body's way of demanding that Jean slow down.) Although she wouldn't put it this way, Jean had become Real.

As a Real woman, Jean had stopped trying to look like a POW, stopped pushing to be the leader and organizer of everything she saw, and stopped denying that she needed time to take care of herself. She learned that, contrary to what she had been taught, emotional pain isn't a terrible, shameful thing. Instead, it's a sign that some part of you needs and deserves attention. This lesson is hard to learn in a culture that is phobic about pain and obsessed with avoiding it. Most women are so ashamed if they feel pain that they try to hide it. Of course, this means that they cannot get support from others. It's only when we take a risk by telling the truth that we learn how well it works.

"The most surprising thing is that once I let people know I felt bad, they actually were more accepting of me," Jean told me as she wiped tears from her eyes. "When I finally admitted I felt terribly sad and lost, I got support in ways I never thought were possible."

It's Not All Depression

The painful feeling that Jean identified first when she became Real was depression. This is extremely common for women. Clinical depression is much more likely to be diagnosed in women than it is in men. In the Object Culture it's common for us to respond to depression by taking medication—Prozac or Zoloft, for example—than to try to move on. But in most cases, depression is a much more complicated issue, and it offers you a chance to gain important insights. If you use the *feel it, face it, fix it* formula, you can see that, like all feelings, emotional pain is a signal.

A Real woman recognizes that pain contains a lesson about life's pleasant and not so pleasant possibilities. It tells us we're out of denial. And even though it hurts to be out of denial, it's also an opportunity for Real women to blossom.

OPO: *Stop whining about life being so difficult and get on with it. When life hands you lemons, make lemonade.*

Toni: *That's a catchy slogan, OPO, and I do believe in accentuating the positive, but no one can learn or grow by ignoring her feelings and just pushing forward. That's why so many of us make the same mistakes over and over.*

OPO: *Women who do that are fools who don't learn.*

Toni: *Calling someone a fool is Thinglish. No one can know something before she has learned it.*

So what do you do when you feel emotional pain? First, it's always important to consider there may be a biological cause—premenstrual syndrome, genetics, thyroid disease, menopause—for your depression. Once you and your doctor have considered this possibility, you can then look at the emotions, experiences, and attitudes that lurk behind depression. Women have a tendency to convert all kinds of emotions, but most commonly grief, anger, fear, and shame, into depression. We do this because those initial feelings can be frightening.

When you are Real, and understand that emotions are not shameful or dangerous but can be honored as guides to a more authentic life, it's easier to examine your emotions. But you have to be alert. Feelings don't always announce themselves clearly. Sometimes you will experience a strange period of blankness, which therapists call a dissociative state (as in disassociated from yourself). This blank feeling may actually be a sign that something you saw, heard, or recalled was so painful that your mind sought to escape it. At other times, you may feel a little twinge of unhappiness. Perhaps your feelings will take the form of a repeated theme in your dreams. Just as important are those sudden desires to eat when you're not hungry or seek comfort in alcohol or drugs. You can train yourself to take note of these signals and respond to them through reflection, talking with someone, or writing in a journal.

Oddly enough, journal writing can produce results

even when you think you have nothing to put down on paper. At those times, you must commit yourself to just keeping the pen moving for ten minutes. Write anything at all, even the phrase "I can't think of anything to write." If you have emotions hiding just beneath the surface of your awareness, they will come out as you move your hand across the paper. These feelings are among the most common that emerge when people are becoming Real:

Grief. You may grieve for the time you lost while chasing the Object ideal, for the relationships you may have missed, for the parts of yourself you neglected.

Anger. Once you realize how OPO and the Object Culture exploit your insecurities, you might feel a significant amount of healthy anger.

Shame. When we become Real, we have to face some unhappy truths about ourselves. Every living person has said and done things that are hurtful, destructive, and dishonest. We all have traits we'd like to change. Recognizing these things about yourself is painful, but you cannot improve while in denial. However, don't confuse feelings of shame with those the culture imposes on you for being different. There is no shame in individuality.

Fear. As demanding and unfair as the Object Culture may be, it promises safety in conformity. Being Real involves taking risks. You wouldn't be alive if you didn't feel a little afraid.

These are just a few of the painful feelings that can arise as we become Real. Because they sometimes echo disturbing experiences or feelings from childhood, they are valuable sources of insight. In my work with therapy clients, I ask them to recall moments in the past when they felt the same emotions. If you recall being ostracized at school for being different, for example, you just might be able to identify the moment when certain seeds of insecurity were planted. These discoveries, paired with your adult perspective and values—which include empathy for the girl you once were—can help you move past the pain. Something good can come out of any pain, especially if it brings you insight into your own Real life.

Coming Out of the Trance

My client Belinda had always struggled to hide a fear of men that was so deep she sabotaged every potentially serious relationship. Before she worked at becoming Real, she had developed the habit of speaking to herself in an inner monologue that numbed her to what had happened in the past and was hurting her in the present:

> "Everyone has trouble in relationships. I'm just having bad luck."
> "You gotta kiss a lot of frogs to find a prince."
> "So many guys are jerks. Where are the nice ones?"

Belinda repeated these kinds of statements to herself in a hypnotic refrain that numbed her to the real causes of her pain. She used such nostrums to protect herself from the fact that her attitudes about men had been affected by repeated painful experiences in childhood with a brother who was four years older than she. Between the ages of seven and twelve, this brother had used Belinda as an outlet for his own rage by humiliating her, punching her, and sexually molesting her.

The key was to recognize that Belinda's self-talk was a form of self-hypnosis that kept her in denial. None of what she said related to herself as an individual. All of it was aimed at casting her life in generalized terms that explained away her feelings. And as long as she clung to the one-size-fits-all assessment of her troubles, she didn't have to face what had happened to her. (Unfortunately, as long as she did this, she wouldn't make progress in relationships, either.)

As she worked with me in therapy and adopted a more Real approach to her life, Belinda began to look behind the generalities to consider what had happened with her brother, and how it had made her feel afraid of men and set the stage for her to ruin every relationship that approached real intimacy.

In Belinda's case, the Real pain of loneliness was a gift. Pain prodded her to enter therapy, get Real, and excavate the source of her fears and self-defeating behaviors. Many of us do what Belinda did, use sing-song, repetitive self-talk to numb ourselves and avoid issues. How can you tell if you are doing this? Give voice to the words that play in your head. If you discover that you repeat Thinglish generalities and clichés like "Always look on the bright side" or "When life hands you lemons, make lemonade," stop and challenge yourself. Before you make that next pitcher of lemonade, let yourself think about the dark side of life you experienced as a child. Give the little girl you once were permission to speak, and resist the urge to quiet her with platitudes that sound like they came out of one of those dolls that produce speech when you pull a string.

When you explore your past, you get a chance to identify the moments when certain seeds of pain were planted. These discoveries, paired with your adult perspective and values—which include empathy for the girl you once were—can help you move past the pain.

One way to gain access to your inner pain is to return to the mask you made in chapter one—and this time focus on the inside of it, the face you don't show to the world.

Inside the Mask

You can use the mask you made in chapter one to help discover and explore some of the historical sources of pain in your life.

Since OPO demands that we present a perfect outside to the world and keep everything unpleasant hidden, let yourself examine the way you decorated the *inside* of your mask. The words, images, and designs likely point to parts of yourself that have been hurt, things that make you feel ashamed or angry, and sources of regret and grief.

Ask yourself:

What sacrifices have I made as I tried to be a POW?

Who/what taught me that the hidden parts of myself were bad?

Was I ever shamed for being my Real self?

The answers to these questions and the feelings you experience as you reflect on the inside of the mask—the inside of *you*—will point to the sources of your pain.

In many cases, simply recognizing the sources of our pain helps us feel better. One young woman I work with had images of acne and the words *stupid* and *fat* written inside her mask, along with a drawing of a gun that symbolized her suicidal feelings. Acknowledging these messages helped her move toward self-empathy, but it didn't eliminate all of her pain.

In *The Velveteen Rabbit*, the Skin Horse said that pain is inevitable. By the time you are Real, your fur may be shabby, parts of you may be loose, and a few pieces may even be missing. But the rewards of being Real are so great that these losses can be accepted and lived with every day. Similarly, some of the pain in a Real woman's life must be endured, but she learns from it, adapts to it, and thrives in spite of it (or perhaps because of it).

Beware the Outside Critics

The inner pain we feel as we become Real is an unavoidable side effect of growth. It tells you that you have evolved past comfort in your current stage of development. For example, every woman feels some anger when she realizes the destructive power of the Object Culture. An angry response to the status quo, especially when it exploits our insecurities and drives us to be POWs, is perfectly normal and almost universal among Real women.

Similarly, unrecognized grief is practically epidemic in a society that shames people simply for crying. Anyone who drops her defenses and honors her innermost feelings is likely to experience accumulated feelings of unexpressed loss.

If these challenges from within were all that women had to face as they become Real, the process would be tough enough. Unfortunately, you may have to confront other sources of pain as you declare your independence from the United States of Generica and have your own Real Revolution. The Object Culture is full of criticism for people who choose the path less traveled. The media often depict us as oddballs and misfits. But these generic criticisms cannot hurt us as deeply as the ones that come from those we consider friends and loved ones.

Women who choose their Real path to happiness threaten the status quo. Some husbands/partners don't like it when their lovers put less time into their appearance and more into their creative passions. Some children think it's "weird" for a mom to go back to school or take up a nontraditional hobby. They may criticize you, complain, or insist that you are embarrassing them. Similarly, old friends can have trouble relating to you if you no longer share mutual interests, like shopping, and suggest instead they join you in community activism or volunteerism.

In some cases, people may be unable to adjust to the Real you. At the same time, you may discover that you no longer feel comfortable with certain relationships. A new, more honest, and empathetic you may not be able to tolerate insensitive or destructive people who once had your easy acceptance. It is a bit harder to endure superficial nonsense once you have clarified your beliefs and decided to truly live by them. I'm not suggesting that Real women must become critics and scolds. But I am saying that it sometimes can be hard to find Real people and Real acceptance.

The twin problems of isolation (you are rejected for being "different") and alienation (you don't relate to others because you actually *are* different) seem to be common among Real women. Both problems are mentioned by visitors to the Velveteen Principles website, and I have experienced them myself. When I do, they motivate me to return to the principles—especially empathy, courage, and gratitude, and I find they make me feel better.

The Real Power of Fairies

It may seem strange to you that I would bring up the subject of fairies as I write about the pain associated with becoming Real, but I have noticed that many of the Real women I know—women who acknowledge that pain is part of a Real life—adopt fairies as inspirations and reminders of the secret, seemingly magical strength all women possess.

For me, fairies are a reminder of the fully alive and Real little girls we all were, before the demands of the Object Culture were heard loudly in our heads and we began to worry about whether we were good enough. Girls of that age are resilient, optimistic, and full of wonder. Like fairies, they are not desperately inhibited. They believe they are worthy and have enormous potential for happiness and fulfillment. They do not live with the pain of judging themselves or being judged by others. They are fierce, funny, active, and mischievous counterculture activists. These qualities are exactly what Real women are hoping to recall and cultivate in themselves when they hang an angel from the rearview mirror of their cars or put a fairy tattoo on their shoulders. Though products of whimsy, and nonbelievers would say imagination, fairies and angels are symbols of what Real can feel like inside. They tell us that we were once spirited, fearless, and free of doubts and fears, and that we can be that way again.

Some themes tend to emerge in women's "fairy fantasies." They relate to feeling powerless, angry, mistrusting, and dismayed with the Object Culture's values. Fairy fantasies also tend to include a wistful desire to be free of *shoulds*. And the caretaking that fantasy fairies perform tends to empower others, create justice, fairness, and beauty.

It is no accident that in Margery Williams's *The Velveteen Rabbit* the appearance of a fairy announces that despite the pain and struggle he has experienced, the old toy bunny has become joyously Real. This is why many Real women keep a fairy or angel or some other symbol of female energy and optimism in a place where they will see her every day. (One woman I know keeps a handmade fairy on the mirror in her bathroom. It greets her every morning and night.) Give your fairy or angel a prominent spot. She'll remind you of the spirited girl who still lives inside you, and that even in its most painful moments, being Real promises a better you and a better life.

If I Were a Fairy

Who were you before the Object Culture got to you? What kind of fierce, passionate, and fabulous person were you? This original, brave, Real you represents your "inner fairy." She still lives in your heart, and she's waiting to be recognized.

How do you summon this creature? Imagine having the qualities of a fairy. You are knowing, impish, creative, and energetic. You have the magic ability to fly and be invisible.

What would you do if you had those powers? Let your mind wander and play with these ideas, and you will find some clues to the Real you. Here are just some examples of what I've heard friends say about what they would do if they had fairy powers to grant wishes, give people what they want, fly or be invisible:

I'd visit men's locker rooms.

I'd give things to people who deserve them, kind of like Robin Hood, robbing from the rich to give to the poor.

I'd see what my boyfriend is like when I'm not around.

I'd go to any concert or ballgame I wanted to, without a ticket.

I'd go to sleep and wake up without an alarm clock.

I'd eat whatever I wanted, whenever I wanted.

I'd spy on sneaky politicians and spread the truth to the newspapers.

I'd slap the people who deserve it.

I'd be as sloppy as I really want to be.

I'd give everyone health insurance.

I'd feed poor people.

I'd take the power of speech away from liars.

I'd watch my family figure out how much they depend on me and miss me when I'm gone.

I'd spy on other people's lives to see if I'm normal.

I'd listen to what other people say about me.

What is your fairy fantasy? What does it say about who you really want to be?

Velveteen

Principle #10

Real Women Are Flexible

Real woman couldn't ask for a better role model than Madeleine Albright. As the nation's first female secretary of state, she held the highest office any American woman had ever achieved. But for me, Albright doesn't stand out because of the job titles she has earned, but because of the traits she has demonstrated in the pursuit of an extraordinary and productive life. At the top of the list is her flexibility.

Having fled to England from Czechoslovakia with her family at the start of World War II, Albright eventually came to the United States as an eleven-year-old, where she was forced to adapt to a completely new culture. After college, she married and had three children, returning to school when her kids were older to begin a career in foreign affairs. After twenty-three years of marriage, when she was forty-five, her husband left her, but she didn't spend much time mired in anger or self-recrimination. Instead, she embarked on a life of study and public service that allowed her to express every bit of her character and intelligence and to do good work in the world.

Of course, Madeleine Albright's talents are extraordinary, but none of them were more important to her than the flexible attitude she brought to her life. She adapted to all of her choices and challenges—immigration, motherhood, divorce, education, career—like one of those great cypress trees on the Pacific Coast; they bend with the wind, but still keep growing. Their beauty is a product of both their inner qualities and their adaptation to the pressures of life.

Time and again I have seen women demonstrate similar flexibility. In my therapy practice, I have worked with infertile women who were desperate to have children, and who found an outlet for their love through adoption. I have seen women recover and thrive after divorce, the death of a partner, or the loss of a high-status job. Others have managed to adapt when their children have needed rehabilitation for addictions or when illness brought disability.

In every case, when women thrive in the midst of adversity, it is because they have allowed challenges, losses, and sufferings to make them more Real—more themselves—and they felt enough self-empathy to be serious and flexible about their responses. Being both serious and flexible are essential in responding to adversity. Setbacks and obstacles give us a chance to find new strengths and abilities. However, we must value ourselves and be willing to practice lots of self-care if we are going to put the energy into rebounding from trauma and uproar. If you can act with Real courage and accept that pain is a natural part of life, recovery is imminently possible. If you cannot, the results can be tragic.

Rigid Women Break

My own mother's life was a tragic example of how an inflexible set of beliefs can ruin a woman's chances for happiness. Just after my birth, my mother learned she had Parkinson's disease. With a rapidly progressing case and little treatment available at that time, she quickly lost movement in her face, developing the telltale "mask" of partially paralyzed facial muscles associated with the disease. Soon she also had trouble walking. But these physical problems were not as devastating as her emotional response.

Instead of grieving her loss, facing her circumstances, and finding a way to continue with her life, my mother chose a kind of waking death. Although I never knew her before her illness, I'm told she had been bright, active, beautiful, and artistic. (Paintings she did when she was a young woman provided ample evidence of her creativity.) With her diagnosis, she became withdrawn, disengaged, and fearful. By the time I was ten years old, she was so ashamed of how she looked and of her physical limitations that she almost never left her home.

As happens in so many cases, one person's troubles ripple out to affect many others. As a young girl, I begged my mother to get a wheelchair so that she could travel more easily outside our home, but she refused. Her explanation was that she couldn't stand to have people look at her as disabled. In truth, what disabled her was her own emotional rigidity. If she had possessed the flexibility to accept her illness and limitations, she could have had a much fuller life in those years. We both missed out.

It is easy to understand how a profound illness brought grief to my mother, but the bigger tragedy was that she lacked the Real resources to recover. This was because she had never challenged the generic definitions she had accepted for her life and never worked at becoming a Real individual. Until she became sick, my mother had based her identity on the Object Culture's definitions of a successful woman. She took pride in the fact that she was tall, thin, and fashionable. For a while, my family had been fairly well off, and this status was important to her. But when these things were lost as she became sick and my father's business faltered, she all but ceased to live.

Looking back on her life, I can see that without a Real sense of identity based on Real values, my mother's losses overwhelmed her ability to cope. Life handed her an enormous Bag of Rocks, and she broke under the weight. However, she was also affected by a common problem that stops many women cold: She was afraid of change. Of course, the prospect of redirecting one's life in radical ways is daunting. But as a result of that fear, some of us do nothing. Shame about the need for change leads to inaction, paralysis, and an inflexible approach to life.

Fortunately, Real flexibility offers an endless number of better options. It also unleashes one of the most important resources we possess—the power to choose what we believe and to make the best of what we have been given. Human beings are uniquely blessed with this power of choice and perception. And every moment of our lives brings an opportunity to use it.

Don't Limit Your Choices

The needle on any compass turns freely across 360 degrees of direction. Each degree represents a path that might lead you away from where you are standing now. The same is true for you as you stand at any point in your life. You don't have to limit your choices to just two directions—for example, the way society defines success and the way it describes failure. There are hundreds of other options if you have the flexible frame of mind that allows you to imagine them.

But don't let the variety of life's choices intimidate you. Often, when we need to change directions, the course adjustment that will take us to a more satisfying life is not all that radical. You might decide to open your own restaurant instead of cooking for yourself, or you want to move from being a student to being a teacher.

New ideas and creations arise only when we depart from the quest for perfection and allow for change. They never come from imitation or copying. Real is original.

A more flexible approach begins with setting yourself free of most of the Object Culture's expectations. Discovery, whether it involves pursuing your own interests or discovering an entirely new avocation, requires that you be open to whatever comes your way. If your only definition of a good first day on the ski slopes means never falling down, then your expectations need adjustment. Let yourself be a beginner. Let yourself change directions, change priorities, and change interests.

OPO: *What is this, the sixties? Sounds like you're encouraging women to be wishy-washy, ditzy, and flaky. Just make a decision and stick with it!*

Toni: *There's nothing gained by hiding from new information and refusing to adjust. Life changes us; circumstances demand that we adapt. You have to be flexible, like a skier who bends her knees as she flies downhill. If she gets rigid, she'll fall.*

Sometimes, interestingly enough, the change a flexible person must embrace involves being more assertive. My client Maddie chose to adjust in this way after running up against some big obstacles at her job. A physical-education teacher in a big school district, Maddie was highly competent and held a master's degree in her field. But because she is very pleasant and upbeat, her coworkers tended to treat her with a fairly condescending attitude. And for a long time she felt compelled to conform to their expectations, always accepting what they said and never rocking the boat.

But there was more to Maddie than a go-along, get-along gal. She had serious questions about the way girls' sports were short-changed in her district—lower funding, lesser facilities—and when her complaints about these inequities were ignored, she worked to develop a more assertive exterior. The next time her supervisor asked why she wasn't her cute and bubbly self, she reopened the matter of fairness for girls and got a more respectful hearing. This wouldn't have happened if she hadn't been empowered by some of the essential Velveteen principles—courage, honesty, self-empathy—and if she hadn't been flexible enough to change her approach in her interactions with others.

Maddie's flexible response required a kind of strength similar to what the practice of the physical discipline in yoga brings to the body. Yoga promotes not just muscle power, but physical flexibility, which is very important to protect us from injury. Real flexibility, which we cultivate in our hearts and minds, promotes emotional, intellectual, and spiritual resilience. When we are resilient, we bounce back after stress or injury, and we keep going even after experiencing losses. Without it, we collapse, as my mother did after receiving her diagnosis, and fall into despair.

Flexibility is most important when it comes to our beliefs, which, as you recall, play a vital role in our feelings and behavior. A flexible woman is willing to reflect on the beliefs she holds about herself and change when necessary. I don't mean we should be wishy-washy or indecisive when it comes to our core values and commitment to being Real, but certain beliefs restrain us and keep us from growing.

Start with the Woman in the Mirror

he outdated, irrelevant, or destructive beliefs handed to us by parents or the Object Culture are not immutable. New experiences teach us new things if our minds and hearts are open to learning. Imagine how much better my mother's life would have been if she could have changed her belief that only her conventional beauty and status mattered, and if she had learned to find joy in expressing the parts of herself that were untouched by her illness and waiting to be shared with others.

How do we engender flexibility in ourselves? We can begin by adopting a broader, more flexible view of what makes a woman beautiful, worthy of love, empathy, nurturing, and respect.

This practice is especially important as time passes, and we all show the signs of aging. Breasts sag as do many other body parts. Wrinkles appear along with gray hair. Bellies that have borne babies or the weight of many decades hardly ever stay flat. These are the Real facts about aging. Denying the physical reality of this process is like denying your need to eat, drink, and breathe.

Yet according to the Object Culture, women become less beautiful, less valuable, and less respected as they age. For this reason we desperately fight time and gravity by obsessing over food, exercising compulsively, spending lavishly on lotions and potions, or undergoing the plastic surgeon's knife. And yet many women still find reasons to hate themselves every time they look in the mirror.

While it's fine to try to look your best, no one should be driven by a sense of shame over losing the battle with age. Time waits for no woman. The Real answer to this challenge is a more flexible definition of beauty, one that includes a deep appreciation of the variety and diversity of our sizes, shapes, and experiences.

Our life experiences show up on our bodies in many forms, from wrinkles and curves to dimples and scars. They represent all the good things we have done, all the laughter we have enjoyed, and all the struggles we have endured. They reflect our strength, our will, and our spirit. There is nothing shameful and everything to love about an aging woman's appearance—and only a rigid and inflexible attitude prevents us from appreciating our bodies at every age.

To develop a new, flexible view of your appearance,

consider revisiting the Beliefs–Feelings–Behavior formula. First, think about what you believe when it comes to beauty and aging. Chances are your attitudes are influenced by the styles of the times. Proof that beauty is a product of culture is plain to see in the way popular images of desirable women have changed over the centuries. One of the oldest images of female beauty ever discovered is a small statue, the *Venus of Willendorf*, which depicts a large, squatty-looking woman with saddlebags, a big belly, and pendulous breasts. This shape, the opposite of today's ideal woman, was once the subject of veneration.

Don't criticize yourself when you discover that you have internalized the conventional standards of today's Object Culture. We all have those messages stuck in our heads. Instead, let yourself consider new definitions of beauty that include the way you look right now. Everything that makes you different, imperfect, and unique is beautiful and reflects the wonderful variety of women's experiences.

Next, add to your self-image the beauty that's evident in the way you conduct your life. There is Real beauty in the empathy, generosity, honesty, and courage you possess. It can be seen in your eyes and in the way you move. It is profound and lasting and grows more beautiful with time.

These beliefs, and others you may develop on your own, could be present in your heart and mind whenever you look in the mirror. They can lead to more positive feelings about yourself, and these feelings will be evident in your increasing nurturing behavior toward yourself and others. The cycle this sets up is a never-ending process that makes you and your life more appealing and inspiring no matter your age or clothing size.

Fortunately, life brings us constant reminders about what is truly valuable and what is not. While I worked on this book, I happened to have an accident while driving my car. (A tow truck, of all things, broadsided me on a rainy Sunday afternoon.) I was rattled but unhurt. A police officer arrived to assess the scene. I'll never forget what he said: "It's only property damage, ma'am—you're okay." As the weeks passed, I realized that so much of what we worry about is only property damage, especially when it comes to the process of aging and the vagaries of beauty. Our outsides, our stuff, our object selves are only property, and we Really are okay, regardless of our crumpled bumpers.

Growth Requires Change

A flexible approach to life requires that we use what we know to change how we think, feel, and act. For everyone, change is the essence of life, and it happens whether we like it or not. Often, in fact, other people are our catalysts to change. Partners, parents, siblings, children, and friends all alter and evolve, and as they do they need different things from us. If we want to love them well, we must be flexible enough to change along with them. For many women, this Reality becomes most obvious when they have children. Kids' need for flexibility is obvious from the start. All babies are different, and if you expect a certain type of child—especially the calm, gurgly, contented kind—but get a different kind—one of the colicky, fussy, demanding variety—you'd better adjust, or you'll make life miserable for yourself and your child.

Parents of disabled children often learn this lesson of flexibility early in the child-rearing process. They recognize that their children are not generic babies, but idiosyncratic individuals. With this in mind, they can truly enjoy every step of their children's particular progress.

Without this flexibility, a parent can't help but communicate disappointment and disapproval. I've seen it happen. One of my therapy patients, a bright, energetic, talkative, analytical, funny woman, was born to a mother who thought that a "good baby daughter" was quiet, docile, and undemanding. Her personality so disappointed her mother (and her mother displayed her disdain from the start) that she learned to hate herself. As adults, these two women have never felt connected, and both feel the loss.

Obviously, children grow better when mothers are flexible. Flexible mothers love the child visibly and continue to love her as she grows. Babies become toddlers; toddlers go to school. With each transition, we must let go of the old and adapt to the new. The big tests generally come in late adolescence, when children demand the greatest acceptance and flexibility. If you are thoroughly rigid and rejecting when your daughter wants a tattoo or your son takes an unconventional job, a chasm will open between you.

At these moments be careful of Thinglish phrases like "No child of mine will ever . . ." or "What you do is a reflection of me!" These old sayings suggest you regard your child as a possession or status Object. If, instead, you can listen to your child, watch her with affection, and regard her as a Real person, you may be able to open your mind and heart to appreciate her individuality.

A marvelous symbiosis occurs in this process. As evolving adults, we pass through stages of maturity and development ourselves. If we parent our children in a Real way, we can become more flexible and open and match their growing need for independence. In the best cases, when our children are ready to be regarded as capable, autonomous adults, we are able to relate to them on that basis. Grown children are far more likely to love their parents in return if they receive respect, acceptance, and empathy.

Of course, mothers with newly adult kids and women who do not have children share the universal challenge of adapting to middle age. Sometime in her forties or early fifties, every woman must recognize she has reached, or even passed, the halfway point of life. It is natural for us to reflect on our lives at that point, on the prospect of our own mortality, and on our priorities for the future.

The good news at age fifty is that women can reasonably anticipate living many years with good health and vigor. The key to Real fulfillment will be found in how you choose to spend those years. You can try to deny the fact that life brings you a finite supply of days. Or you can respond to this truth by treating each moment as a valuable and perishable gift.

For some, midlife can bring a sense of urgency, to which they respond with dramatic decisions. If you Really need a new career, a new home, or even a new relationship to give meaning to the future, you won't be alone. Some women experience breathtaking changes during their middle years. But for many, the answer is not a sudden break from the established patterns of life, but a flexible reshaping.

Flexible women reject the notion that any single period represents "the best years of life" and choose, instead, to believe that every stage of life can be filled with meaning and purpose and rewards. With this in mind, Real women will take some risks in order to grow in midlife. They will go back to school, try a new job, or take up a new activity that they have long been too scared to try. Although not quite as dramatic as a death, divorce, or a move to a new city (cases in which we are literally forced to be flexible), these self-directed changes will provoke a reaction from all the people who were comfortable with how things have always been. But a loving partner, husband, or friend will help facilitate the change without being threatened. In fact, if a change makes you happier and more Real, those intimate people in your life will celebrate the difference with you.

This is not to say, however, that the world will bend with you through every transition. The Object Culture takes special pains to control and direct some life changes. When a woman's husband or other loved one dies, for example, she will be granted a limited period for mourning. In the United States of Generica, death is a failure, a reminder of reality beyond our control. For this reason, many people want to move past it quickly. After a few months, some will start talking about how it's "time to move on." At the same time, those who have suffered a loss will begin to feel ashamed of their sadness and try to cover it up. A similar dynamic takes place around illness in a land where everyone is supposed to stay young, healthy, and beautiful. Women who become sick or disabled often notice that relationships wither, and feel they lose status.

The flexible alternative to accepting the culture's rules involves making your own choices. You don't have to erase from your conversations a loved one who has died. Talk about him or her as much as you need to and in the way that feels Real for you. If friends and family won't listen, there are clergy, therapists, and groups who will. The same is true for women who have gone through an illness, like cancer, or are coping with a disability. No law in the realm of the Real requires that you hide what happened to you.

Indeed, if you want to live as a Real woman, empathy—for yourself and others—may lead you to be open about who you are and what you have experienced. Although aging is a wonderful, enriching process, loss is an inevitable part of it. This is why people in the disability rights movement refer to those with perfectly functioning bodies as TABs, Temporarily Able Bodied. Age takes something from every one of us. Women who adapt to the challenge and simply go on with life as well as they can often discover they feel even more liberated from the demands of the generic culture. When the U.S. of G. rejects you for your imperfections, you can become even more Real and create a life that is even fuller and more specific to you. One of my favorite stories of adaptation as an approach to life involves violinist Itzhak Perlman, who got polio as a child and has ever since needed leg braces. At one concert he broke a string on his violin during his warm-up. Rather than leave the stage and delay the music, he signaled the conductor to begin. Somehow he managed to bring new sounds out of the remaining strings and complete a wonderful performance. After the concert, and a long ovation, he told a local reporter, "You know, sometimes it is the artist's task to find out how much music you can still make with what you have left."

Women's Flexibility Advantages

adeleine Albright once said, "I've learned that there is absolutely no formula for being a woman. Women's real advantage is that our lives come in segments due to biology, and we can do a number of things."

Indeed, biology does grant women permission to change and take on different roles, and we are expected to do so. Maybe this is why women often seem to respond to personal crises and the prospect of change better than many men do. The men I know suffer more keenly from a job loss or divorce than my women friends. We simply seem better equipped to adapt and move forward.

The reason for this seems to be in our tendency to define ourselves—our interests, concerns, and the things we value—much more broadly. Recent social surveys on the world of work have revealed a variety of findings that support this belief. Women, it turns out, are far less motivated by money. We place more value on time with the people we love and are likely to choose careers that give us flexible hours, so we can be more involved in the other aspects of life.

Of course, these choices are influenced by the central role women play in family life. (We are still expected to be the primary caregiver for children.) But these responsibilities are not our only motivation. While men tend to be driven more to achieve at work at the exclusion of other interests, women tend to take a more holistic approach to life. We factor in the value of good relationships, a secure home, and a nurturing community. And because of our biology, we also understand that our roles will change over the course of our lives. Time teaches us that we must evolve.

One possible result of this approach to life is that women may be less vulnerable to major shocks. Men who identify themselves with work can be devastated by the loss of a job, a demotion, or even a small setback. Women who gain a sense of self from many different sources don't lose as much when things go sour in one area. I would argue that our diverse sources of Real meaning and connections make us more resilient. In short, you can be Really flexible.

Velveteen

Principle #11

Real Women Find That

Love Endures

s he was dying of lung cancer, one of my
husband's close friends leaned on a filing
cabinet at the office where they worked,
looked over a vast area of cubicles where people were
bent over computers, and said in a rasping voice, "You
know, all of this stuff we do here is bullshit. When
you get to the end, all that really matters in life is love.
You think about the people you have loved and the ones
who loved you. That's all there is in the world that
really matters."

This basic truth, that love matters most, lies beneath
most of the deepest concerns we express about our lives.
We might talk about our frustrations and anxieties, but
the subtext is generally about loneliness and the need
for love. This is evidenced in the community forums on
my website, Velveteenprinciples.com. If you go there
you'll see nearly all of the questions and conversations
have to do with love in some form. Every woman is hoping to be loved for her Real self.

Real love is out there, but it doesn't come to us easily.
Here, as in so many other areas of life, the Object
Culture interferes. It wants us to stay frozen in place,

always insecure and underdeveloped, so we continue to strive, compete, and buy things in an attempt to feel better about ourselves. But, of course, this isn't the pathway to the kind of love that considers who we truly are and nourishes us as individuals. In order to get that kind of love, you have to be willing to show your Real self to the world. And sometimes that can be hard.

Be Loved for the Real You

When Fran, a woman I have counseled, started to work on her undiscovered, Real self, her husband, Jack, was initially supportive. He wanted her to be happy. But the awakening that comes when a woman abandons the POW model can be rough. Examining her life, Fran found much that she didn't like. Her job as a bookkeeper was boring. She felt like a slave who did all of the upkeep of her home. And her sex life with Jack—when they had time for it—was humdrum. When she began to explore her options, Jack resisted.

Not surprisingly, Jack felt threatened by Fran's rather

ruthless inventory of her life with him. For a few weeks, she seemed unhappy with everything. Worried and defensive, he asked for a couples counseling session. When we were all together, he complained, "She's changed. She's not the girl I married. I don't know what she wants at all."

The problem, as Fran saw it, was that Jack believed he could take one specific action—say something, do something, buy something—that would satisfy his wife and return their lives to where they had been before. For her part, "I don't want him to get me something," Fran said. "I want him to get me!" By that, she meant she wanted him to understand her, appreciate her, and love her for the unique person she is—and was becoming.

Every Real woman desires to be loved as a unique person. Nothing feels better. Conversely, she feels uneasy if she realizes that her partner is loving her in a generic way. The classic example of this problem is generic sex. When someone loves you like an Object, with techniques that feel like they came out of some manual on how to please a woman, it's impossible to enjoy sex.

As you read this, you may be nodding your head and thinking about how your lover, male or female, fails to love you as a unique and specific person. Certainly

Fran had this feeling. But before you put too much blame on your husband or partner, consider the perspective Jack shared once he understood what his wife was talking about.

"I've always wanted to know more about what Fran cares about and wants," he said. "But sometimes I feel like she's hiding from me. I have to guess what she is looking for, and that's when I wind up doing what everybody says you're supposed to do—buy her things and do stuff around the house. That's what everybody says a woman wants, and if she doesn't tell me different, that's all I can do."

Fortunately, Fran and Jack valued their relationship. The more Real Fran became, the more determined she was to find ways to connect with her husband. They succeeded, but not after exploring both the old generic ideas that held them back and the new possibilities that were available to them as a Real couple.

Ditching Notions of Perfection

In lieu of any Real understanding of what his wife wanted, Jack had approached love according to the generic responses offered to us by our culture. He had lots of clichés to choose from. Romantic love is such a compelling theme that most cultures develop strong myths about how it works. All of these are based on unRealistic expectations. One that has been especially troublesome in the lives of women I know is the *Beauty and the Beast* scenario.

In this fairy tale, a generically gorgeous woman with no discernable talents other than charm is somehow able to recognize the potential for good inside a beast who is otherwise unattractive and alienating. She tolerates his negative behaviors until her tenacious love for him turns him into the prince he was meant to be. She proves he was only a beast in disguise. Her love transforms him. He becomes the ideal mate—adoring, wealthy, and attractive. All she had to do to bring out the best in him was put up with a little abuse.

On a very superficial level, the story of *Beauty and the Beast* teaches us a positive lesson about tolerance and looking beyond appearance to see the soul of a person. But this applies only to the man in the story. Like every other fairy-tale woman, the "beauty" is shown to be good and deserving because she is pretty. Her superficial beauty and generic form of loving behavior are so powerful they can make a man into a perfect partner.

Sadly, women who are not connected to their Real selves can fall into the *Beauty and the Beast* trap. Many factors set women up for this scenario. Two common antecedents are low self-esteem and previous experience with abusive men. Women with such problems don't believe they deserve partners who treat them well, but they nurse the dream that they can transform a beast. In twenty years of working with women in relationships, I've never seen a beast become a prince. But I have seen cases where the beast emotionally abused, physically battered, and even murdered the beauty.

Beauty and the Beast is, of course, just one of the many fantasies and misconceptions women cling to in hopes of finding the generically perfect love of their lives. Like men, women often look for superficial qualities, searching for someone who is a hunk, a stud, a hottie, or a catch. Once these status elements are fulfilled, women then adopt some fairly unRealistic beliefs. These are among the most commonly held beliefs:

> My husband/partner is perfect. (Or I can make him/ her perfect.)
> I am perfect for him/her. (Or I can become perfect.)
> We can be everything for each other.
> This relationship will make me happy for the rest of my life.
> If my partner loves me, he/she will automatically know what I want.

You could add your own list of unRealistic beliefs to the ones above. And the number of fantasy scenarios we can build out of these beliefs is almost limitless. Besides *Beauty and the Beast,* I'd say the next most common fantasy is what I call the "Bait and Switch," where women enter into long-term relationships with men whose apparent wealth, status, and good looks make them seem larger-than-life fabulous in the beginning, but as sure as a well-crafted car advertisement can lure you to buy a lemon, relationships built on such superficial beginnings become very costly.

In all fantasy-based relationships, women make the mistake of believing that a partner is or can be a perfect Object for our love. We forget that "perfect" is neither possible nor desirable, and we guarantee ourselves sadness and grief if we believe it is. In fact, whenever someone seems to be perfect, the truth is that we just don't have enough information about him or her.

The fantasy of perfect is most destructive when we base our relationships on those generic, ideal Object qualities that are inevitably subject to change. If we connect on the basis of Object values, we feel genuine panic over the prospect of our partners' discovering our flaws, so we engage in the exhausting pursuit of perfection. Women, in their attempts to defy the changes nature brings with age, have actually died from eating disorders and complications related to plastic surgery. Both men and women sacrifice their mental and physical health by overworking to maintain their wealth and status.

In the complex dance of expectations, people involved in Object relationships may even get locked into a competition. We monitor our partners. They monitor us. When we spot a flaw and complain, we win. When they identify flaws in us, they win. The same thing happens when people disagree. They allow themselves to argue, then try as hard as they can to "win." Framing a discussion in terms of "winning" and "losing" is classic Thinglish. So is the act of placing blame on others or ourselves. A Real, revolutionary alternative leads couples to a mutual understanding and greater empathy rather than positions of winning and losing.

What drives us to struggle against inevitable and humanly acceptable change? In many cases it's a faulty belief that only our bogus appearance of Object perfection makes us worthy of love. Women who live by this assumption inevitably attract partners who share this belief. Many of these partners, especially men, are profoundly affected by the false images of women in the media. Portrayals of women with unnatural bodies lead many men to expect the same from the women they know. Failing to understand the effect of these unRealistic expectations, they feel let down and disappointed and may look elsewhere for what they have been trained to want.

Tragically, in these Object-based relationships, women live with the knowledge that if they deteriorate physically or if a new, shinier woman/Object comes along, then they may be replaced. The stakes in this game grow higher all the time as the media present ever-more-perfect bodies—even porn star versions of beauty—as the ideal that women must meet. Who isn't going to feel insecure if she's supposed to simultaneously defy the march of time and constantly upgrade herself?

A similar insecurity affects women who climb the social ladder by attaching themselves to someone with money and power while ignoring signs of potential problems with their values and character. If they achieved this position through some superficial means, women may unconsciously feel unworthy of their new status and are reluctant to speak their minds when problems arise. How many women put up with infidelity, addictions, neglect, and even abuse because they value the status and material comfort they achieved through marriage?

In the struggle to maintain a "perfect marriage," women will also sacrifice their own identities. I was struck to read, once, what the former wife of an internationally renowned athlete had to say in a very candid description of her failed marriage: "If you aren't careful, it (marriage) can tempt you to become a 'yes' woman for the sake of salvaging your romantic dream. It can lure you into a pattern of pleasing that will turn you into someone you'll hardly recognize and probably won't like."

The potential harm done by unRealistic beliefs about love—especially when we base a relationship on Object values—grows worse with time and multiplies when children come along. For this reason, it is absolutely essential that women understand their value, self-worth, and expectations before they commit to a lifelong partner. If you have developed your own set of beliefs that help you to be Real, then you are likely to prize someone with similar values. With these values in mind, you may discover that your "type," the kind of person you are likely to love, is based not on appearance or status, but on deeper characteristics. Instead of "tall, dark, and handsome," you are more likely to "fall" for someone who is "empathetic, flexible, and generous." Which type of partner is more likely to join you in an enduring love?

Custom-Made Love

When Jack and Fran began talking openly about their relationship and their own expectations of love, they were shocked by what they discovered. Fran revealed that she had tried obsessively to comply with a generic definition of beauty, believing this would please Jack, while she hid her own desires to be less artificial and more authentic. In the process, she hid her Real self and thereby guaranteed that she wouldn't be loved for who she Really was.

For his part, Jack talked about the idiosyncratic young woman he had met and married. He said that she was feisty, artistic, opinionated, and passionate. "I never wanted a generic wife," he insisted. "But Fran seemed to just fall into that role with me, and it got worse when we had kids."

When couples lose their sense of individuality, they conspire together to destroy the attraction, excitement, and passion that brought them together in the first place. It can be easy to let this happen. Modern life is very demanding, and it takes effort to listen to each other and adapt as our partners change. But when you fail to invest in your Real relationship, then confusion, disappointment, anger, and resentment grow. These feelings, and the grief associated with losing that unique connection to a life partner, can lead to arguments or emotional withdrawal, both of which can destroy a relationship.

The alternative, one that is chosen by nearly every happy couple, shifts the focus from superficial goals to a set of specific and shared values that allow a couple to build a custom-made relationship.

This is not a simple matter. Couples who defy social stereotypes are often criticized and misunderstood. A flexible man is "henpecked" or worse. An assertive woman is trying to "wear the pants" or worse. But isn't it illogical to assume that we will all create relationships that fit a single template? How could there be just one way for couples to negotiate a life together?

If every individual is unique and imperfect, the same must be true for the relationship formed when two unique and imperfect people come together. Real people make mistakes, reveal flaws, and even hold beliefs that contradict your beliefs. It is easier to accept these truths about your partner if you know that when it comes to true values, you stand together. (As Antoine de Saint-Exupery wrote, "Love does not consist of gazing at each other, but in looking outward together in the same direction.")

Most couples in Real, lasting relationships share these ideals:

Mutual empathy—Partners respect and honor each other's feelings, experiences, and dreams.

Mutual support for growth—When you love someone, you want them to follow their interests, dreams, and aspirations, and develop in every way.

Courage—Sometimes you have to be brave if you are going to defy Generic Ideals and develop a one-of-a-kind relationship. Others, including friends and family, may criticize your choices.

Honesty—Your partner cannot supply support if you are not honest about your strengths, issues that challenge you, and your most cherished hopes.

Mutual generosity—Real love moves us to give. In lasting relationships, partners take turns making sacrifices and accepting help.

Commitment—When couples are Real, the practice of empathy, mutual support, courage, honesty, and generosity prepare us to weather the inevitable crises in relationships and life.

In Real relationships, the observation "You've changed" is a positive, even joyous comment. Men and women in love want their partners to develop. They change in tandem, and it is this constant evolution that inoculates them against boredom. As they embrace change, Real couples also acquire the flexibility to endure through hard times.

When Fran and Jack began to make a custom-built

relationship, they started by renewing their commitment to each other and talking about how they might grow as individuals and a couple. When Jack felt certain of Fran's commitment to him, he found it easier to listen to her talk about how unhappy she was with, among other things, her job. He supported her effort to leave her bookkeeping job and start a tax and business services company. It wasn't as dramatic a shift as Jack had feared, but it was enough to make Fran feel as if she was setting her own course rather than following a path laid down by someone else.

The happiness Fran felt as she grew with Jack's support made it easier for them to approach other issues as a couple. Feeling as if Jack "finally got me," Fran allowed herself to be more open sexually. When she talked about wanting the occasional day spent entirely in bed, it turned out Jack liked that idea. And when she explained to him that he didn't have to be quite so tentative and restrained, sex became more exciting and spontaneous than it had ever been. Their renewed empathy for each other made sex all the more exciting because they received so much joy in pleasing each other.

I'm not claiming that Jack and Fran embarked on a two-person sexual revolution that stayed at a fever pitch all the time. No couple can maintain that kind of intensity on a permanent basis. But they developed deeper trust that made sex better. And this trust also spread to other parts of their relationship. Fran no longer resented when Jack took time for golf and sailing. Jack was willing to do a little more work around the house because, like Fran, he felt recognized and appreciated as an individual involved in a unique relationship.

Over the long term, when a relationship lasts a lifetime, Real love helps us to accept each other's flaws and adapt to aging. One couple I know quite well serves as a marvelous example of this. Robert and Lydia were married more than fifty years when she died at age eighty. In their time together, she had seen him through alcoholism and career struggles. He had helped her cope with several serious illnesses. This couple had a unique and mutually supportive relationship that no outsider could fully grasp. Their enduring bond prepared Robert to accept Lydia's changing health, to learn new skills for caretaking, and to find satisfaction in this role. When she died, his grief was soothed by the knowledge that together they had helped each other make the most of the gift of life.

Real Love and the Single Woman

lthough much of society seems to promote the idea that life must be organized around a marriage or other intimate relationship, this is a very limited definition of fulfillment and happiness. When you are Real, you know the error in such sweeping assumptions. Life comes in infinite variety, and most of us will live without a partner for long stretches of time. Some of us choose to live as singles; others haven't found a partner who fits. And Realistically speaking, some of us may not ever happen upon the right mate.

Fortunately, your Real values can guide you to more empathetic and flexible forms of love in all sorts of relationships. When siblings, friends, and relatives love each other more Realistically, they do not require absolute agreement on every issue. They do listen with patience and respect. They allow for differences and even take pleasure in seeing life from someone else's perspective. (Imagine, for example, what you can learn about yourself by hearing your sister's recollections of life in the same family.)

Because Real, enduring relationships require trust and tend to evolve slowly, they are precious and somewhat rare. When a woman says she's got "a dozen best friends," don't believe her. In my mind, there is a big difference between a Real friend and an acquaintance or a friendly neighbor. Real friends demonstrate Real love and commitment to each other over time. It's not a casual thing. In *The Velveteen Rabbit*, for example, Skin Horse stands by Rabbit through every adventure in the nursery. He also supports his friend in his pursuit of being Real, even though it means Rabbit will leave him behind.

In the end, the only heart you are fully responsible for is your own. But as obvious as it may seem, many women overlook *themselves* as they think about lasting, enduring love. Before we can connect with others, we must be able to regard ourselves with kindness and understanding. Fortunately, it's never too late to develop the kind of self-empathy that gives us the strength and energy to move through life, grow, and relate to others.

Remarkably, I have seen women develop high personal regard and become fully Real, even as they were suffering the pain of a lost relationship. Whether it's through death, breakup, or divorce, the end of a seem-ingly close relationship inevitably leads us to self-evaluation. If, in that moment of crisis, you can con-sider something new—say, rejecting Object values and adopting a Real perspective—you may be able to see yourself in a new light. And if you can regard yourself with empathy, you'll renew and increase the possibil-ity that someone else will notice and love your Real self, too.

Some Very Sexy Principles

Have you ever noticed that even with all the lights, cameras, and make-believe action, most of the sex depicted in the media seems flat and unexciting? This is because media sex is the ultimate expression of Object relationships. Everything about it—the bodies, the moves, the expressions—is mechanical, generic. In contrast, sex between people who are Real and enjoy a Real relationship can produce both the emotional connection and physical pleasure that suit lovers perfectly.

When it comes to the Realness of loving and making love, the principles explained so far in this book—and the following two principles—align themselves nicely with our intimate aspirations. Of course, everyone will have her (or his) own ideas about how the principles that help us to be Real can work for us when it comes to love and sex. But to get you thinking, I offer the following suggestions:

Principle 1. You Can Be a Real Woman

Real sex that is custom-made to please you and your partner is possible, too.

Principle 2. Becoming a Real Woman Is a Process

Real sex is a process, too. It's not a game with a goal (i.e., it's not all about the orgasm), but a dance that is dynamic and evolves over time. What pleases us at age twenty may not be appealing decades later.

Principle 3. Real Women Are Emotional

A great many emotions, including raw lust and a hungry need for pleasure, are definitely part of Real sex. But don't forget that emotional attachment and feelings of safety can open the erotic floodgates.

Principle 4. Real Women Are Empathetic

Great lovers are able to put themselves into the minds and bodies of their partners and almost feel their pleasure. It's how they get it "just right" at the perfect moment.

Principle 5. Real Women Are Courageous

In the trusting realm of Real love, you bravely talk to your partner about what feels good, and you try new things.

Principle 6. Real Women Are Honest

When love and sex are Real, you can be honest about your emotions and what does and doesn't feel right.

Principle 7. Real Women Are Generous

Empathetic women value their partner's pleasure. They are also generous with themselves.

Principle 8. Real Women Are Grateful

When you can express a little gratitude for a wonderful lover, you invariably get more attention and appreciation. Praise anything that feels right!

Principle 9. Real Women Experience Pain

True love does not always run smoothly. When you are Real, you know that things don't always work out, but the off nights don't ruin a relationship. Maybe you wanted sex, but your partner didn't. Maybe something happened that felt weird to you. It may be difficult to talk about sex. You may feel vulnerable. But Real women bravely talk things through even (and especially) when it hurts.

Principle 10. Real Women Are Flexible

Admit it: For a minute your playful mind flashed on a woman who is so physically flexible she can get into very wild sexual positions. There's nothing wrong with physical agility, but being flexible also means being understanding, receptive, and open-minded.

Principle 11. Real Women Find That Love Endures

Real sex can endure, too, just as long as we are healthy enough and connected emotionally. Yes, even older, less-than-perfect-looking people can enjoy themselves sexually.

Principle 12. Real Women Are Ethical

It almost goes without saying, but let's say it anyway: Real sex never involves violations of trust, integrity, and privacy.

Principle 13. Real Women Have Lives Filled with Meaning

Real sex means much more than orgasm. It means deep, abiding love that helps us feel safe and encourages our growth.

Velveteen

Principle #12

Real Women Are Ethical

What do I care if he's married?
He's not married to me!
That's her problem!

—OVERHEARD AT A CAFÉ

I face a classroom of students, mostly women, and ask them to raise their hands if they consider themselves to be ethical people. Of course, a group setting creates some pressure to say yes. After all, who would reveal themselves to be unethical to others? But my students' unanimous claims to having ethical values also reflect the findings in surveys and polls. We all consider ourselves to be ethical.

A deeper truth emerges when I pose a second question to my class: "Is anyone here using a pen, a pad, or a pencil taken from the supplies at their workplace?" Amid the chuckles and sideways glances, every person in the class eventually raises a hand. And for the next hour and a half, we engage in a lively effort to define and understand what it means to be ethical in our daily lives.

Many of the ethical choices we face are far more complex and present us with much greater consequences than our behavior in the office supply closet. For this reason, we tend to ignore or deny important issues and never develop a set of standards or ideals— call it an "Ethical Sense"—that will lead us to reliable choices and behaviors. And when we start looking for guides, we can be confused by competing religious beliefs and philosophies. However, stripped down to their essentials, most ethical codes share certain eternal elements familiar to anyone trying to be Real. These "higher values" include empathy, compassion, honesty, courage, responsibility, and integrity.

In the Object Culture, these qualities are generally set aside as we are urged to chase fun, wealth, beauty, and status. On those rare moments when the United States of Generica considers matters of ethics and character, women are reduced to stereotypical expectations. For us, being "good" and "ethical" is all about the important but softer values of caretaking, compassion, generosity, empathy. Integrity, courage, and responsibility remain the domain of men, rarely mentioned when we consider the ideal woman.

Nothing can diminish the value of empathy-based ethics and behavior. When women show compassion and act to benefit others, we demonstrate Real morality and make meaningful contributions to the ones we love and to the larger society. Where would we be without a mother's desire to put her children first? But what about the other side of the ethics equation, the one that requires integrity, courage, and other strengths? Aren't they also part of a woman's ethical sense?

Of course they are. Without them, women are considered "nice" but not "trustworthy." We are labeled "kind" but "weak." It can be easy to accept this status, living our days as "nice" and "kind." But if we settle for this incomplete definition of ourselves, we can never develop the kind of Real character that would allow us to be fully ethical people in the important areas of life, from family, to work, to community. And we certainly can't attempt the very first step toward developing a complete ethical sense: learning to ask questions.

Question Everything

Perhaps the biggest threat to ethical behavior is the Object Culture's promotion of what social science professionals call "groupthink," a set of ideas and attitudes everyone unconsciously conspires to accept. Groupthink often fosters unethical prejudices and allows for little variation. It encourages conformity and pushes us to abandon unique and creative thoughts. Going along and getting along are rewarded, while those who don't go along can expect to be ostracized, criticized, and marginalized.

Being ethical is hard, and often, surprisingly, it can make you unpopular. Ethical behavior can be particularly difficult for women who are trained to please everyone and never to make others uncomfortable. We are under special pressure to conform and stay quiet even when we discover something unethical occurring. Sometimes a woman's opinion is discounted by people who say things like, "What does she know? She's only a woman." In other cases, a woman who speaks up may be labeled a bitch (naturally!), hormonal, and/or crazy.

Although it takes strength, Real women can develop and enact their own ethical standards, and avoid the effects of groupthink by using the power of questions.

When we stop and ask questions, instead of automatically conforming, we can make room in the decision-making process for our own values. Sometimes this is a matter of challenging a big social stereotype:

TV says all women soothe emotional trauma by eating ice cream.

Everyone looks good in pink.

Every woman must have a baby.

Women are the weaker sex.

Are these ideas really true? You can get to the facts by asking: Who says? What's the evidence? Do those assumptions apply to me?

As we question the conventional wisdom of the Object Culture, we can readily identify the problems with one-size-fits-all ethical standards. Because people and life's experiences come in infinite varieties, stereotypes are never foolproof. But in other instances, the effects of groupthink are more insidious, and breaking its influence means asking questions of yourself.

Melanie, a very kind and decent woman I have worked with, had been employed at the same computer software company for fifteen years when a newcomer, who happened to be Asian, was promoted to management ahead of her. Although Melanie had been ambivalent about the job opening, and the managers had sensed she wasn't much interested in having more responsibility, she resented her colleague Anne's success. On a subsequent visit to a nearby city, she found herself in an Asian neighborhood and felt angry and hostile about the people she saw there. Stereotypes ran angrily through her mind until she stopped and noticed her thoughts and feelings.

At the night class on ethics where we met, Melanie was courageous and honest enough to talk about her resentments and anger, and how they seemed to have spread from an individual she knew to every person with Asian roots. "I know this is screwed up," she said, "and I think I know where it came from."

Although she had never discussed the issue anywhere else, Melanie told the class she had been raised in a family that condoned bigotry. Although ethnic and racial slurs were avoided, many casual conversations with her mother and father had included references to "those people," which meant any so-called inferior and different ethnic groups.

"Now I know that when I was a kid it wasn't my fault that I thought this way, but once you know, once you're aware that you are doing it, it's your own responsibility, and I know the way I'm thinking right now is pretty unethical."

Melanie was right about every point she made, except the last one. Yes, she had fleeting bigoted thoughts. But her decision to question her own attitudes, re-examine what she had learned as a kid, and own up to it were the essence of ethical behavior. She had a firm set of values that left no room for bigotry. She also had the integrity to recognize that her responses were in conflict with her values.

The final step toward a new understanding of herself and her coworker came when Melanie began to examine more closely her resentments about the promotion of her coworker. Anne had been open about wanting more responsibility and won the new job fairly. Also, Melanie could see Anne was struggling with all the demands that came with the position. With just a little empathy, she could recognize that the benefits Anne received were outweighed by the price she was paying in stress. Soon

Melanie's feelings matched her ethical beliefs, and the bigotry she had felt evaporated. Because she knew that possessing ethics was a process—one that she practiced successfully by asking herself questions—she didn't feel she had failed. The struggle to make choices that match our ideals is the essence of ethical behavior.

Questions are useful ethical tools in many circumstances because they help us think more deeply and reflect on how our actions make us feel about ourselves. For example, when women have affairs, they are often troubled by conflicting emotions. Most have justifications for their actions: A partner strayed or they feel neglected. And yet they also feel tremendous guilt. When these women ask themselves questions about these feelings, they invariably discover that their guilt is a signal. It tells them they have betrayed their higher ideals. Understanding that this pain is the result of a self-destructive act, they are far more likely to take responsibility for their ethical lapses.

The self-questioning technique works in less dramatic circumstances, too. You can use it, for example, when a neighbor who works for the cable company offers you a free connection to the network. Ask yourself what will happen when you turn on your "free" TV every night. Will you feel like you have betrayed your own values? And how would you feel if your children understood that you were taking something that didn't belong to you every single day? Make these kinds of questions part of your ethical process, and you will reach the answers you need. (By the way, "Do as I say, not as I do" is not ethical parenting. We cannot expect more of our children than we expect of ourselves.)

Avoiding the Risk of Absolute Certainty

The opposite of Melanie's ethical approach to her brief run-in with prejudice—questioning her own feelings—is the kind of absolute certainty that makes it impossible for us to take in new information, learn, and grow. For example, if Melanie had not questioned her bigoted response to Asians but instead hid her feelings or stubbornly justified them, she would not have resolved her inner conflict. Since prejudice conflicts with her higher ideals, she would have felt shame and guilt for as long as those feelings persisted.

On a global scale, we all understand that great evils—invasions, holocausts, segregations—have been carried out by people who are absolutely certain that their actions are justified and ethical. Remarkably, much of the damage done in everyday relationships is also the product of actions by those who feel completely justified. We all know people who seem thoroughly certain about every opinion they hold, and base their actions and relationships on these certainties. In extreme cases, these very-certain people develop long lists of definite standards for right and wrong, and believe that these highly detailed rules guarantee they will be correct all the time.

If you are Real, you do have certain nonnegotiable standards. You value empathy, courage, and honesty, for example, and you won't tolerate abusive or intimidating behavior. You may also stand firm on a host of other values, including fairness and mutual respect in relationships.

But if your ethical sense also includes generosity and flexibility, you will feel reluctant to impose your specific choices on others. Instead, your ideals will be a basis for making your own decisions, not a justification for bullying and judging others.

In this complex and varied world, individuals have the privilege to make a variety of choices as long as they do not harm or impose on another person. We are all free to choose where we live, whom we love, and which passions we will pursue. If we try to impose on others our detailed beliefs about these kinds of things, they are bound to resist and will eventually stop communicating with us. This occurs with alarming frequency in families, especially when parents are adamantly certain about what is right and wrong for their adult children.

Ultimately, ethical absolutes carry such power that they must be wielded with great care. We can be absolutely certain about what is right for ourselves. But when it comes to others, most differences can be respected and accepted. Is it Really ethical to demand that others accept all of our beliefs?

Virtue and Women's Character

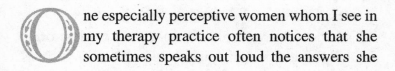

One especially perceptive women whom I see in my therapy practice often notices that she sometimes speaks out loud the answers she seeks in her quest to be Real. The problem is, she delivers her wisdom to others and doesn't always let the message apply to herself. "Sometimes all you really need to do," she says wisely, "is attend your own lecture."

Most of us would do well, as we search for our Real ethical values, to attend our own lectures. This is because most of us already know the basics of right and wrong. People all over the world share universal ideas that represent what is good in human nature and behavior. Experts in axiology, the study of values, generally recognize certain universal virtues drawn from religious and secular sources that are so ingrained they are practically part of our DNA. I offer them here as a starting point for those who want to think deeply about what they value most.

Tolerance	Faith	Prudence *(practical wisdom)*
Honesty	Hope	Justice *(fairness)*
Flexibility	Love	Self-knowledge
Self-reliance	Moderation	Devotion
		Fortitude *(moral strength)*

The above list is hardly comprehensive. Most of us would also add certain universal moral beliefs such as the Golden Rule—"Do unto others as you would have them do unto you"—and several of the Ten Commandments, especially those that bar killing, theft, adultery, and bearing false witness. These are all helpful, but because every formal ethical system has its limits, we each must make our own lists of personal virtues and values. As we struggle to live by these ideals, we show others, for better or worse, the content of our character.

Although difficult to define, character is demonstrated by the choices we make, in public and in private. When we are deliberate about making our actions consistent with our highest values, we can develop a habit of ethical behavior that demonstrates strong character.

Fortunately, character can be developed and improved over time, like a muscle that grows with focused exercise. The same is true when it comes to integrity. As we make considered, ethical choices over and over again, we develop strength of character, and we demonstrate integrity. Both of these traits make us more trustworthy, and allow us to contribute even more to the greater good.

But don't expect good character or ethical standards to make you a perfect, automatic, do-the-right-thing machine. We all naturally need time to respond to problems, listen to our hearts, and decide on a course of action. Try to have faith in yourself and where your conscience will lead you. A recent study of whistle-blowers (people who call attention to covert problems inside organizations) found that their decision to tell the truth about wrongdoing can take many months to be enacted. It also found that people are able to overcome their fears and act because their desire to live in a manner that is consistent with their values is such a powerful motivator.

Ethical Leadership

In one major part of life—parenting—women have traditionally shown strong character and what could only be called an ethical leadership style. We have been the ones charged with teaching children right from wrong and making both safety and justice Real in our homes. In our families we also have had the opportunity to promote Real values and challenge the Object Culture. By creating a Real climate, we can encourage the best in others.

How do we do this? Proper role modeling is one way. Another way is making sure our actions match our values. Ethics are in what we do, consistently, over time, not just what we say we believe. Are you an ethical mother? What are you modeling for your daughter? If you're raising her to believe she is a princess, how will she take care of herself? Maybe she'll find a prince, who knows? But sometimes, as we know, princes turn out to be frogs and leave for a new princess. Or they die. Or they become disabled or unemployed. How will your princess handle life if these very possible events occur? Mothers who practice Real ethics model self-sufficiency for their daughters and teach them to believe in their own Real capacity for growth and learning. If we constantly fret over our appearances and seek happiness through shopping, we signal to children, partners, and everyone else watching us that these elements of life are most important. But if we live our lives as Real women, we demonstrate the possibility of thriving outside the Object Culture. Going another way requires that we show strength and courage from time to time. We can stand up for what we value and speak out when we see violence, exploitation, and dishonesty.

Considering how much women have contributed to

family life, to both children and partners, it's ironic that we have not generally been expected to play the role of ethical leaders in our communities and workplaces. However, in recent years the Real strengths of women have gained recognition as important elements of ethical leadership. Indeed, case studies have found that successful leaders generally show remarkable levels of empathy (especially during crises), are gifted listeners and communicators, and model important, Real principles.

It turns out that the best leaders are the ones who are able to win the trust of others by demonstrating over and over again that they are guided by Real values. The most respected leaders are ethical, and they create an environment that allows people to be creative and pursue their passions in ways that are good for the individual as well as the group.

It's important to notice that the ethical leadership of Real women is not a soft and mushy thing. When a leader has spelled out the values she takes as her standard, she can be ethically strong about enforcing them. Human flaws and mistakes deserve understanding and forgiveness. But certain inhumane actions—cruelty and exploitation of others, for example—cannot be tolerated.

History is full of inspiring examples of women leading by this kind of Real, ethical standard: Rosa Parks in Montgomery, Jane Addams in Chicago, Margaret Chase Smith in Washington. But the history books don't have room for all the women who have bravely stood their ground or led others. It happens every day when a teacher stands up for a student in need, a community group comes together to solve a problem, or a worker chooses to do the right thing instead of going with the flow.

The Real women I know have been guided by an ethical sense that helps them to consider their choices in light of their values. Although their ideals are humane, generous, and infused with empathy, these women are not afraid to be firm when it's required and to fight—for themselves and others—when it's necessary.

OPO: *Who am I, Mother Teresa? It's not my job to fix the world. I'm not perfect. I can't repair everything.*

Toni: *Being ethical doesn't demand perfection. There's no such thing. Why are you so defensive about this?*

OPO: *Maybe I don't feel good enough to offer*

anyone anything, or I'm afraid no one will ever help me.

Toni: *Everyone has something to give, even if it's just respect or a smile of affirmation.*

In reality, ethical leadership is rarely about making dramatic statements or waging epic struggles. More often such leadership is practiced one-on-one. Opportunities for this kind of leadership are everywhere. Do you know a young woman, perhaps a teenager, who needs someone to talk to? The young can be difficult and hard to understand, but try anyway. Adolescence is where the pain of objectification is first felt. Let a young woman feel your empathy. Imagine how your life might have been improved if a Real woman had done it for you.

In every corner of life we can find opportunities to express our ethical values. And if you open your eyes, you will see women doing this everywhere. In Chicago, for example, I recently stumbled onto an inviting café that fed my appetite, my mind, and my heart.

Diners at Hilary's Urban Eatery are welcomed by a sign that says, WELCOME, LEAVE NEGATIVITY OUTSIDE. The walls are decorated with hand-made art and the words *Sincerity, Humility, Courage*. One piece hanging on the wall proudly declares "Imperfect." Menus are emblazoned with the Latin motto *Lux mentis lux orbis*, which means "light of the mind, light of the world." Add a warmhearted staff, and the delicious food served at this café becomes part of a meaningful and memorable experience.

The eatery's founder created her business to achieve very distinctive goals. Her ethical sense led her to make an environment that was peaceful, inspiring, and amusing. She made the place comfortable and secure for her workers and was careful to balance her own needs with those of her workers and customers as she set her prices. The result is a very successful business with a loyal following and a happy place to work. As Hilary shows, women can express ethics in every aspect of life. This practice is a natural outgrowth of living Real, and it is the ultimate expression of our desire to be guided by values and to consciously honor our own ideals. Our choices in life don't necessarily become easier under these conditions, but when we make our ethical standards part of the equation—when we operate with this intention—we cannot betray ourselves. This is one of the great rewards Real women reap.

Velveteen

Principle #13

Real Women Have Lives

Filled with Meaning

hen I was the little girl sitting on the rock, posing as my parents snapped a photo, I faced a future constrained by the tyranny of low expectations. My parents, and the larger Object Culture, expected nothing more of me than marriage and a generic life devoted to taking care of my husband, children and, ultimately, my aged mother and father. This was the program communicated to me throughout childhood and confirmed as my family sent me away to college where they expected my main occupation to be finding a man.

I was not alone. Generations of women have been subject to this training and confined by very narrow definitions of what it means to be a woman. For most of time, women have been forced to express their individuality in the most subtle and secret ways. Otherwise, they could be criticized, punished, and/or abandoned.

I was fortunate to come of age in a period when many women questioned the longstanding, generic definitions of success that emphasized Object-oriented roles and traits. Women wondered aloud whether it was enough to be kind and beautiful helpers. And they questioned whether achievements in certain limited areas—giving birth, keeping house, parenting—were their only options. The point was not to denigrate these aspects of life—they will always be important—but to consider whether they should be the only or best options open to all women.

At stake in this debate, although few people understand it this way, is the search for meaning in life. Whether we recognize it or not, of all the struggles we endure and the efforts we make, the important ones are concerned with attaching a higher value—a meaning or purpose—to our existence. Far more than acquisitions, beauty, status, or mere happiness, meaning makes our lives full, satisfying, and complete.

One true example of this vital principle is a friend of mine who was abandoned as a child and raised in foster care. Throughout her adult life she has been a volunteer for children's charities—including one devoted to kids dying of cancer. Even as a child, Linda had figured out that she could choose to live by certain values—she emphasized generosity, forgiveness, and integrity—and that these would help her make proper choices about matters both big and small. She was right. She chose always to forgive hurts, to be generous toward others, and to stay true to herself.

"Things just sort of fall into place when you adopt a generous and forgiving attitude," she once explained to me. "You find you get the chance to make friends, help other people, and feel good about yourself. When I look for meaning in my life, I think it's got something to do with being able to add something positive to someone's life and letting them add something positive to yours. We're here to help each other through, I think, to help each other get the most out of our time here."

Without knowing it, Linda was living by a philosophy much like the one that guided Mahatma Gandhi, who coined two of my favorite sayings: "Be the change you seek in the world" and "The best kind of politics is when you help other people become their own best selves."

Of course, the values-driven choices made by Linda and other Real women will sometimes appear naïve and impractical to others. (As the Velveteen Rabbit story says, those who are not Real may not understand, and that is the case with the most cynical people we meet in life.) At its most extreme, the Object Culture reduces life to Thinglish clichés: "He who dies with the most toys, wins" and "Life's a bitch, then you die." And if you resist this way of looking at life and seek to access its larger dimensions, you'll likely make others so uncomfortable they will criticize you for "overanalyzing."

But truly, all people seek a sense of purpose or direction in their lives. Some of my most discouraged therapy clients say things to me like "If I died tomorrow, it wouldn't make any difference." And at some time in our lives we all ask, "Why am I here?" There is nothing grandiose or inappropriate about seeking an answer. In fact, it can make the difference between living fully and just existing. When I notice that this most-human desire is being denigrated, I have to wonder why the critic is threatened by the idea that we each may find a purpose beyond striving, acquiring, achieving, and competing.

Two Methods

ometimes we are able to see the values, motivations, and meanings of our actions and choices *after* they have been made. This is common when women use psychotherapy as a tool for understanding. We explore our feelings and past experiences and then discover clues to the present.

In the "Aha!" moment, a woman who was abused or neglected as a child can suddenly see she has fled many relationships out of fear. Another, who was denied a proper education early on, comes to understand why she's so driven to excel in school.

You can examine your own life and discover the meaning in most of your big choices. To do this, you might want to consider writing a brief biography of yourself, one that reveals both your passions—the things in life that excite you—and how you spend much of your time. Answer these questions, and you will have clues to the values that matter most to you and give you a sense of meaning.

In some cases you will see the Velveteen Principles at work in your relationships, career, even hobbies. However, you will also see other purposes—some that make you uncomfortable—at work in your life. At one time or another, each of us has been driven by forces such as excessive ambition, object lust, and jealousy. There is no shame in this truth. No one's perfect, and no one should be condemned for responding in perfectly human ways.

I call the process for finding meaning described above as "excavation." This is because it involves digging deep into the past and into your own values to discover veins of meaning. When you do this, you will find consistent themes. This should not come as a surprise. Every step we make in life is linked to what came before and sets the direction for our future. Meaning is found in each little moment. It can also be found in the most difficult challenges that come our way. Every experience, even the death of a loved one, can teach us something about our purpose, even if it is just that we should value every day we are alive.

If you examine the life you have lived so far and conclude that you have sometimes pursued conflicting purposes, you might want to consider the second method for finding meaning, one focused not on digging up the past, but on acting in the present based on your own Realness. This method involves making more deliberate and careful choices guided by values that you have chosen in a conscious way. If you accept my use of the word "excavation" to describe the backward-looking process, then you might consider the word "gardening" to describe this other, forward-moving method.

When we act as gardeners of meaning, we actively select the values that will serve as our guides, planting them in our hearts, so they may influence our decision-making process every day. As we do this, we begin to define ourselves as individuals and establish that we have Real value, no matter what the Object Culture may say.

The Velveteen Principles make for a nice crop of ideals, but, of course, every woman must make her own list. It can help to actually write them out on paper, along with whatever goals you may have. This is sometimes called developing a "mission statement." Whatever you call it, the process of stating values and then seeking ways to express them as you go through each day instantly makes the meaning of your life more clear.

OPO: *What am I, the United Nations? Next you'll want me to appoint a committee to run my life.*

Toni: *You don't need to be an institution to take your life seriously. Don't you deserve the attention, the consideration that a mission statement implies? POWs may be satisfied with a generic agenda—to be rich, thin, married—but Real women want more.*

OPO: *You can never be too thin or too rich!*

Develop a Mission Statement

Often the difference between a person who finds fulfillment in a Real life and one who does not is a matter of definitions and planning. Women who become Real generally start by defining the notion of a meaningful life for themselves through a mission statement. This will take into consideration who you are and who you hope to become, then sets you on a path to your best life. Don't panic, you don't need to hire a panel of expert consultants the way large corporations do when they're devising a mission statement. There's a fairly straightforward formula.

Mission Statement = Values + Methods

The choices for the first part of the mission statement—a list of values—are endless. Here are the most common:

• **Authenticity:**
Real women are true to themselves.

- **Creativity:**
  Real women express themselves.
- **Generosity:**
  Real women give of themselves.
- **Real Love:**
  Real women are loved for who they Really
  are and love others in the same way.
- **Honesty:**
  The truth matters to most Real women.

If you have trouble defining your own values, take some time to think about women you admire. They can be women in your own life, women you have seen from afar, even figures from history or characters in novels. It doesn't matter where you find them. What matters are the values they express in their lives that you can adopt for yourself.

The second element of a mission statement— the plan for using your values—must be completed if you are going to take the journey to being Real. This may require research. If your vision of your Real self involves learning and teaching, for example, it's not enough to just imagine what that life would be like. You must also find out what's required to become what you dream of being, whether it's a teacher, coach, or anything else. Find people who know the facts, books that give you hints, and other sources that point the way.

Don't restrict yourself to finding work or a career that fits your values. Include all parts of your life in the mix—self-care, relationships, hobbies, etc. They can all be arenas for the expression of your mission statement.

Once you have your mission statement, post it somewhere conspicuous, so you will see it and be reminded of its elements on a regular basis. At times you may notice that your life is out of balance with your mission statement. For example, you may put so much time into seeking money that you neglect your commitment to relationships. Don't punish yourself for straying. We all wander a bit through life. Just make adjustments and get back on track.

Finally, allow yourself some flexibility. The mission statement isn't permanent. I know one young woman whose first mission statement focused on becoming a professional basketball player. As she got older, and fame and wealth lost their luster, she changed her plan to include becoming a mentor to young female athletes. Her mission statement grew with her, and this dynamic brought her an ever-more-Real life.

Ultimately, most of us use a combination of "excavation" and "gardening" to find and then increase the sense that our lives have meaning. When I was a young woman, my sense of purpose was guided by a visual image of a pebble thrown into a pond, which created ripples in the water. I was the pebble, and I hoped that the ripples, which represented my actions in the world, would have a positive effect on others.

Later in life I thought more deliberately about the values that became the Velveteen Principles, and they came to describe in more detail my hope for the meaning of my life. I discovered a profound sense of liberation in this code of values because it gave me a set of standards for making choices about important issues. Doubt and confusion recede when we know what we stand for. This doesn't mean we will ever reach perfection. *I* am far from perfect, and there are times when the steps I take do not match my intended life's purpose. But with the principles in my mind and heart, I have a path to follow toward greater meaning.

Revolution!

One of the biggest lies of the Object Culture states that women must confine themselves to limited roles, curtailed ideals, and downsized dreams. When you are Real, such limitations are unacceptable, and you come to see your life as a unique work of art. Your relationships, experiences, values, and work—among other things—all go into this creation. This process of creation, or journey, is your individual pathway to meaning. It is, ultimately, a trail you blaze yourself. Because we each proceed in our chosen directions, the options are infinite. They also change over time.

When I was a young mother, my purpose in those years was raising and protecting my daughters (as well as enhancing my education and mental health). Now that they are older and more independent, my purposes have changed to include projects like *The Velveteen Principles*.

If you carry your mission statement with you, the choices you make in life will contribute to an overall sense of purpose and meaning. This will happen in an almost automatic way. And at almost any moment, if you pause long enough to look closely, you will be able to see the many elements that give you a sense of meaning. As you grow older, you may recognize how your focus and purpose grow. You may also be able to see meaning expressed in the lives of those you know, most especially in those you love.

When a woman's idealism, higher values, and sense of purpose are evident to all, she somehow becomes more beautiful in our eyes. She expresses these values in what she says and does. Her life is an example of Real living, and she nurtures what is Real in the people she meets, whether they become lifelong friends or passing acquaintances.

As time passes and Real women grow into wiser,

more experienced, and genuine human beings, they serve as role models for a life filled with meaning. Because of one of the great tragedies of our time, the increasing separation of the generations (the old retire to separate communities and extended families scatter), we need women who have led long, Real lives to show us the way.

My friend Bea, the one who went to Harvard in her tenth decade of life, is perhaps the most Real woman I know. Bea found meaning and purpose in her life when she was a young woman mothering a perilously sick child. She promised God that if her boy recovered, she would devote herself to other sick and needy children. When her prayer was answered, Bea kept her promise, becoming a foster mother of sorts to all kinds of younger people who needed her help.

For as long as she could, Bea welcomed those who needed her into her home. But this generosity was not the only proof that she was Real. Although she never pursued a formal career and never gained wealth or fame, Bea was one of the most engaged people in her community. She was a volunteer, an activist, and a leader.

A lifelong learner, Bea helped to found a school of

continuing education at a prestigious Ivy League college, where she was both a student and an educator. Through illnesses, the loss of her husband, and a move to a senior residence, Bea continued to grow, develop, and remain flexible. And when getting out of the residence to experience life became more difficult, she brought the world to her—by helping run a lecture series that became a centerpiece of social life in her community.

In one visit with Bea, which came after she had been in the hospital for several weeks, she talked about returning to school, wondering aloud about transportation and how she might manage a walker in the hallways. It didn't matter whether she would make it back to school or not. What mattered was her desire to learn, develop, and both connect and encourage others.

Bea would be the first to tell you that no one ever reaches the point of perfection and that living as a Real woman can be painful at any age. (She might also find praise embarrassing.) But her deep interest in others, which shines in her eyes, and her determination to live as fully as she can indicates she has something more beautiful and inspiring than perfection. Because she committed herself to certain ideals and never let go, she has a life that has been filled with meaning and purpose. She is the pebble that has been tossed into the water and sends ripples of empathy and inspiration washing over innumerable lives. This is the ultimate reward of being Real—a life that matters. No woman could hope for more.

"I suppose you are Real?" said the Rabbit. And then he wished he had not said it, for he thought the Skin Horse might be sensitive. But the Skin Horse only smiled. "The Boy's uncle made me Real," he said. "That was a great many years ago; but once you are Real, you can't become unreal again. It lasts for always."

We're all ears . . .

. . . and we love to hear Real comments
and Real stories from Real readers.
To share your thoughts, please e-mail the author at
toni@velveteenprinciples.com

INDEX

Index